Village in SURREY

Rosemary Bryant

COUNTRYSIDE BOOKS
NEWBURY, BERKSHIRE

First published 1997
© Rosemary Bryant 1997

Revised and updated 1998

All rights reserved.
No reproduction permitted without the prior
permission of the publisher:

COUNTRYSIDE BOOKS
3 Catherine Road
Newbury, Berkshire

ISBN 1 85306 481 5

Designed by Graham Whiteman
Maps by Lionel Larcombe
Photographs by the author

Produced through MRM Associates Ltd., Reading
Printed byWoolnough Bookbinding Ltd., Irthlingborough

Contents

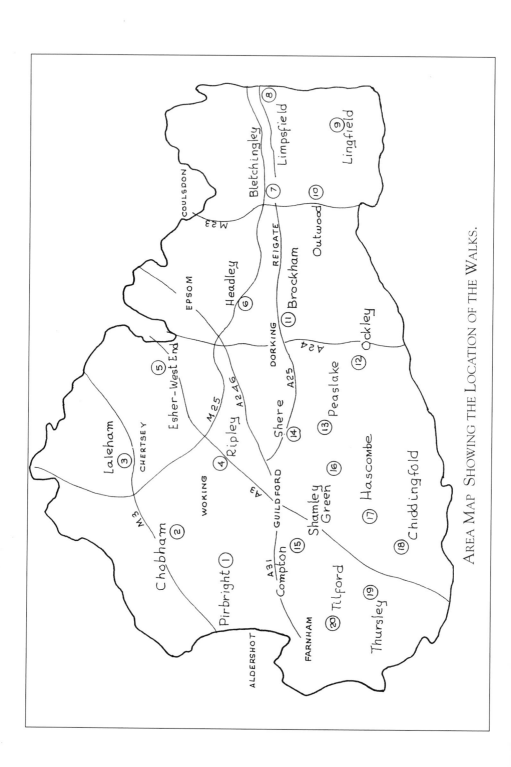

AREA MAP SHOWING THE LOCATION OF THE WALKS.

WALK

Publisher's Note

We hope that you obtain considerable enjoyment from this book; great care has been taken in its preparation. Although at the time of publication all routes followed public rights of way or permitted paths, diversion orders can be made and permissions withdrawn.

We cannot of course be held responsible for such diversion orders and any inaccuracies in the text which result from these or any other changes to the routes nor any damage which might result from walkers trespassing on private property. We are anxious though that all details covering the walks are kept up to date and would therefore welcome information from readers which would be relevant to future editions.

Introduction

Surrey, standing on London's doorstep, cannot be said to have hidden or remote villages but it certainly does have very many hidden and beautiful places only to be found by those who wander quietly on foot to explore the very varied countryside that this small county offers. Over 2,000 miles of public rights of way plus many acres of open heath and common lands make such exploration possible. Surrey is also a heavily wooded county, with hills and steep valleys helping many parts remain hidden from those who do not leave the highways and providing constant surprises for those who do. The villages chosen may each be well known but their variety may surprise you and the walks invite you to explore the countryside that has shaped the livelihoods of those who have lived there over the centuries. Most of the towns and villages were settled in Saxon times and as you walk it is easy to sense how this long history is part of our present and that we too are part of the story as we explore these quiet places.

Several markedly different terrains provide varied walking. Running right across the county are the chalk hills of the North Downs, continuing in the east from Kent and becoming a narrow ridge, the Hog's Back, running into Hampshire in the west. North of this the land slopes into the London basin while south is a more complicated landscape of hills and steep valleys, also running east to west. This area is sandstone, much of it Lower Greensand, with acidic soils supporting large tracts of lowland heath, sometimes referred to as 'Surrey's Last Wilderness'. It's a very special habitat, distinct from upland heath and of international importance. Much of what remains is in Surrey, and areas of wetland and mire, as at Thursley, are Sites of Special Scientific Interest. The Greensand Way, a long-distance walking route starting in Haslemere on the extreme west of the county and continuing for 55 miles over the higher ground to Limpsfield Chart on the Kent border, ranges across 'The Surrey Hills', including Leith Hill, Holmbury, Hascombe and the Hindhead area. These village walks encounter the route in several places for some of the loveliest views are from these hills and the well-drained sandy soils make it good underfoot all year round. The views are generally south over the wide open area of the central weald, heavy but fertile clay stretching away across Sussex to the South Downs. Three rivers with their flood plains and water meadows provide yet another landscape. The Wey and Mole both flow northwards to join the Thames and the walks include stretches of each as well as the pretty Tilling Bourne, a tributary of the Wey, in its valley between the chalk Downs and the Greensand Hills.

A variety of occupations and trades besides agriculture have flourished at different times but many have been those pursued in a fairly solitary way by family groups alongside smallscale farming on the often poor soils. This has given rise to scattered communities, isolated dwellings and small hamlets among the hills and over the Downs, rather than the archetypal nuclear village of fertile lowland areas. Chiddingfold on the edge of the Wealden clay was the earliest centre for glassmaking in England and later had many iron foundries. Both industries made use of the woodland for fuel and water power to drive the hammers and bellows. Potteries and brickmaking, wood and charcoal production, fulling and paper mills, gunpowder and cloth manufacture, mining of the various sandstones as well as traditional village trades such as corn milling, blacksmith, shop or inn keeper have all left their trace. The heathland so typical of the Surrey landscape was formed over centuries by clearance, grazing, cutting of bracken for bedding, and gathering of wood and turf for fires. Now much of it is lightly wooded or scrub covered but grazing is being reintroduced at several sites. However, it is the big city which first drew people out of the countryside to earn a living, then with the help of the railways and better roads drew them back to dormitory towns and villages. As Cobbett so graphically put it, 'it is the destructive, the murderous paper-system, that has transferred the fruit of the labour, and the people along with it, from the different parts of the country to the neighbourhood of the all-devouring wen.' For those caught up in a 'murderous paper-system' these walks should refresh and stir their rural roots.

The villages then are varied. On the one hand it has been observed that there are few areas in Britain where roads and settlements have been confined so largely to the top of ridges. These formed natural routes to the South Downs and the coast before the central areas were cleared but the barren nature of the land tended towards scattered and isolated communities as at Outwood or Headley. More fertile country was cleared and settled along the lower slopes of the hills as at Shere, Compton or Ockley. Other villages grew up along roads as at Ripley or Chobham while others farmed the fertile river plains as at Brockham. There are Iron Age forts on the hill tops and 20th-century defences along the river valleys. All these can be explored via the footpaths and bridleways used over the centuries in the everyday lives of these communities; they are our heritage, enabling us to continue to appreciate and enjoy the countryside around us.

The maps have been carefully drawn by fellow rambler Lionel Larcombe, to whom I am indebted for advice, encouragement and help in checking the routes. The numbered paragraphs refer to the map numbers and used together should help you find your way safely. Also given are details of the relevant Ordnance Survey sheets, both Landranger (1:50 000) and Pathfinder (1:25 000) series, with a grid reference (GR) for the start of the walk. These maps are useful for checking and varying your route and also identifying the main features of views.

One word about parking – readers are respectfully asked to use the utmost discretion when parking their vehicles. Car parking locations are indicated in the text, but if they are full, or for some other reason unusable, please ensure that you park your vehicle in such a way as not to be a nuisance to those who live close by.

If this book encourages you to venture a little further afield that will be good. If it starts you on your own quiet exploration of our countryside that will be better still.

Rosemary Bryant

PIRBRIGHT

Length: 3 miles

Getting there: From Woking 5 miles on the A324; Guildford 5 miles on the A322 and B3032; Aldershot 6 miles on the A323 and A324.	**Parking:** Designated area on the green alongside Lord Pirbright Hall.	**Maps:** OS Landranger 186 Aldershot and Guildford; Pathfinder 1205 Farnborough and Aldershot (GR 945561).

The view across the green and pond to a mix of old houses, shops and two pubs is a peaceful one despite the closeness of busy military towns. Several buildings are 16th, others 18th or 19th century, but all have interesting histories, changing their function to suit the times. Before the hall was built a marquee here sheltered those watching 'moving pictures'. Farms, dame schools, butchers and bicycle shops have come and gone but importantly there is still a post office and a few shops keeping this village 'alive'. Beyond the cricket ground the green merges with the heathland of Pirbright Common.

A village was here in the 12th century

FOOD and DRINK

Head for The Shop on the Green to enjoy coffee, tea or perhaps hot chocolate. You can sit outside or in a pretty room upstairs with fresh flowers on the tables. Coffee comes piping hot in a cafetiere and quiche with a salad or toasted sandwiches are available as well as cakes and pastries. Telephone: 01483 481090. The White Hart, facing the green, has a long history. The oldest part is said to be the remains of an ancient lodge recalling the time when it stood within the Royal Hunting Forest of Windsor. Now it is a comfortable pub, part of the Big Steak House chain with a wide menu. There's a garden where children are welcome, tables on the front courtyard and many quiet corners inside. Telephone: 01483 472366.

sale in the village in aid of church funds.

THE WALK

❶ From the road junction with traffic lights cross into School Lane. Beyond the village school, opened in 1871 before attendance became compulsory, and just after Nettlefield turn left down a drive between holly hedges. Continue until the broad square tower and narrow needle spire of the church come into view. The 'chapelry of Perifrith' dates from the 12th century and was well placed between points of pilgrimage such as Waverley and Chertsey Abbeys and Newark Priory. Church Cottage on the right is Tudor, built on chantry land known as 'torch plot'. Was it a place of shelter for travellers and distant parishioners in this then bleak spot as Yool suggests? To see the church and the memorial to Sir Henry Morton Stanley turn in at the churchyard gate to a quiet haven scented with honeysuckle in early summer. Admire the church tower built of local sarsen stone and notice the inscription 'W.F.1785' and other carved initials. Setts of this hard sandstone have been used in Guildford High Street and Horse Guards Parade. Stanley's grave is beyond the church to the left of the path near the furthest gate, marked with a huge block of Dartmoor granite. Returning to the path, reach the road over a small footbridge.

but despite all the changes its scattered population would have remained isolated in this area of heathland until the 19th century. Then roads were improved and in 1840 the railway opened. In 1852, the London burial grounds being overcrowded, the London Necropolis and National Mausoleum Company took over 450 acres of heathland while in the 1870s another 3,000 acres became a training ground for the Brigade of Guards. Pirbright was now 'on the map' although these developments have kept the surrounding heathland from being built upon.

The walk visits the lovely Georgian church of St Michael where Stanley, the explorer of 'Dr Livingstone, I presume' fame, is buried. It is reached along an old lane that may have been a route for pilgrims to Chertsey Abbey. Various old farmsteads and cottages are discovered and finally a brief visit is made to the cemetery with the Brookwood Memorial and the War Graves. A booklet The Day Before Yesterday by Helen Yool gives an interesting account of Pirbright's history and is on

❷ Turn right and soon go left over a stile. Immediately turn right parallel with the road to a stile and gate near Apple Tree Cottage. This former farmhouse is over 400 years old. Rejoin the road to the end of the garden and paddock and turn left onto a footpath by a fingerpost. Follow

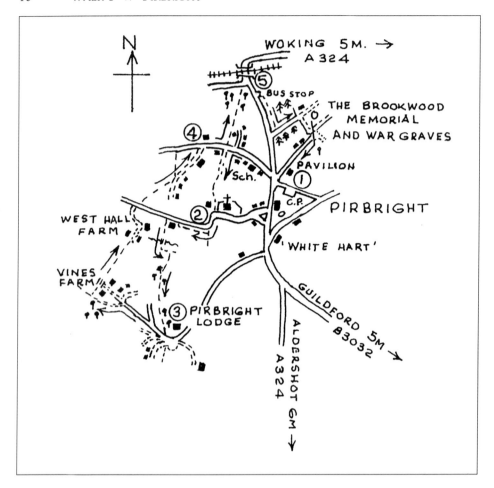

this over a footbridge and then a stile into a field and make for a wooded knoll ahead and to the right. Cross a stile at the top into a field with wide views over wooded countryside. Head to the right of the trees and alongside a stone wall, climb a stile to re-enter woodland and descend beside a fence, crunching beech masts underfoot, to a lane. This is the boundary of Pirbright Lodge, formerly Mount Byron, built in 1774 by Vice-Admiral Byron, the poet's grandfather.

❸ Turn right along the lane and follow the sign ahead for Vines Farm, past the turning to Springfield Cottage. At a clearing where the lane branches, turn sharp left onto a bridleway which soon bears right and continues to a junction of paths beside farm buildings. Turn right on a bridleway past the farm entrance and go down between fences towards West Hall Farm. A memorable evening walk with a setting sun, young calves in the pasture and rabbits scuttling all ways. At a metal

The Brookwood Memorial.

gate keep forwards, bearing right through the farm buildings, with the farmhouse on your right, before swinging left beside a clipped holly hedge to a gate and minor road. Cross to a bridleway and reach a clearing by West Heath Cottages, built in 1880. Go left on a track alongside the common and glimpse the delightful Tudor Wickham Farm House before reaching School Lane. Causeway Farm opposite is another Tudor building although much altered.

❹ Turn right for 200 yards to the 'School' road sign then turn left into the woods. Keep a straight course and emerge by a road junction with traffic lights and a small arched railway bridge. Beyond is the Basingstoke Canal, once a busy place with

---

PLACES of INTEREST

The Brookwood Military Cemetery, an information sheet for which is available from the Canadian Records Building on the left of the entrance. **The Civilian Cemetery**, the biggest cemetery in Britain, is described as 'a bizarrely beautiful place, like a huge deserted park' and has a fine collection of mature trees. The Brookwood Cemetery Society provide a guided tour at 2 pm on the first Sunday each month, with different themes. Telephone 01276 857292 or 0181 6791078 for details. Either walk through from the Military Cemetery or drive to the main gates along The Pales from where the tours depart.

a wharf where coal arrived for the village. Private railway stations were built for the London Necropolis Company at Waterloo and two within Brookwood cemetery. A special train ran each day to convey the coffins and attendant mourners.

❺ Turn right to the bus stop and cross to the layby opposite. Go through a gap in the bushes and turn right to pick up a path running through the woodland parallel to the road. Reach a drive bordered by Scots pine and turn left down to the gates of the Brookwood Military Cemetery. Go through a metal kissing gate at the side. On the right is the simple and elegant 'Memorial To The Missing' in a peaceful setting beautifully maintained and planted to provide something of interest all year round. There are many areas in the cemetery which you may wish to visit but to complete the walk go over to the right-hand corner and through a gate in the fence by a traffic sign. Turn right and in a few yards join a small roadway leading to the sports pavilion and the green near the car park.

CHOBHAM

Length: 5½ miles

Getting there: From Bagshot 4 miles on the A322 and A319; Chertsey via Ottershaw 6 miles on the A320 and A319; Woking 3 miles on the A3046. Exit the M25 at junction 11 or the M3 at junction 3.	**Parking:** Well-signed free car park at the north end of High Street near black and white, timbered Cannon Cottage (see map).	**Maps:** OS Landranger 176 West London or 186 Aldershot and Guildford; Pathfinders 1189 Bracknell and Ascot and 1190 Weybridge, Esher and Hampton Court (GR 975618).

Bustling and busy, Chobham says very plainly that it is just an overgrown village. The church dates from 1080 and with its well-kept churchyard and attractive wooden porch, possibly from Chertsey Abbey after its suppression by Henry VIII, it is the focus of the High Street which has many interesting shops and old buildings. The cannon near the car park commemorates a visit by Queen Victoria to review her troops.

The walk is a gentle one through meadows and beside streams where in early summer the hedgerows are laden

FOOD and DRINK

In the High Street parts of the bar in the Sun are believed to be 500 years old. This friendly inn has a changing menu of reasonably priced bar meals and a cosy atmosphere. Telephone: 01276 857112. Saddlers Halt, by the village exit from the car park, is ideal for tea either in the tearooms or the pretty, secluded courtyard adjacent to the Antiques and Collectables shop. Telephone: 01276 855808. En route Fairoaks Aerodrome Coffee Shop is open from 9 am to 4.30 pm daily for drinks and light refreshments. Telephone: 01276 857700.

with May-blossom and there are buttercups, Milkmaids and Stitchwort. Fairoaks Aerodrome is passed where there is always some light aircraft activity. You can relax and watch this from close-quarters while visiting their coffee shop. Then comes a stretch over wooded heath to one of several fish ponds in this area before returning along field paths.

THE WALK

❶ Leave at the rear of the car park and walk forward past a tree with a yellow marker to a path alongside the cricket field. At the end of the field go left over a stile. Follow the right-hand field boundary to the corner and through an overgrown opening to the next field. Continue ahead with a hedge right. A well-used path joins from the left and continues, via yellow markers, through a series of meadows. Keep forward by a fingerpost at the end of the fourth meadow across a small plank bridge. In the next meadow, with the hedge still on the right, the path swings left then turns right by two oak trees. Stay alongside the hedge and look for a stile approached by a few stepping stones.

❷ Over the stile turn diagonally left to reach a hedgerow by a three-way fingerpost. Go over the stile ahead then diagonally right, crossing a ditch on a plank bridge, to the top left corner. Cross another stile into a lane, turn right and almost immediately fork left, following yellow waymarks along a twisting woodland path to emerge at a junction of tracks. Cross the footbridge ahead into a field and bear left towards trees. Go through a gate to your right, across another plank bridge and out through a stile/gate to a metalled track. Turn left, passing Fox Vane stables, and reach a road.

❸ Turn left, passing two little ponds flanked by yellow iris in summer with moorhens swimming busily. Don't miss Chobham Farm on the right, a delightfully proportioned house with thatched outbuildings draped with wisteria. After a slight rise go left over a stile by a letterbox at the entrance to Trotters Lane. Keep left, crossing a fence where indicated, and follow the hedge to a path in the far corner leading between a hedge and wall into a garden. Go forward with a tennis court left to a fingerpost and through a hedge into a field. Cross to a fingerpost and fence then head for the right-hand corner of the next field to reach a road. Turn left past a bungalow, Frogs Leap Farm, and after a couple of bends come to a hump-backed bridge over the Mill Bourne with the pretty 18th-century Emmetts Mill beyond.

❹ Turn right before the bridge onto a footpath alongside the stream, with Himalayan balsam, Jack-by-the-wall,

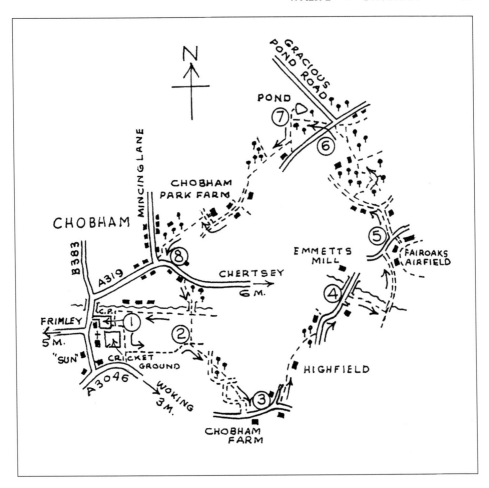

Lady's bedstraw, and a pretty little vetch in summer. At a path junction leave the stream and go left over a footbridge onto a bridleway skirting Fairoaks Aerodrome. Reach the A319 road beside an entrance to the aerodrome and turn right along the verge to the main entrance. (To visit the coffee shop turn into the main entrance and follow signs over to the left.)

5 Go up the private road and bridleway opposite through an avenue of oak trees. Where it divides go left for about 100 yards and, immediately after passing houses on the left, turn right by a finger-post onto a path going up through woods. As the ground levels, turn left onto a narrower winding path and reach a bungalow just past a track coming in from the right.

Fairoaks Aerodrome.

With the bungalow on your left go forward on a broad track through woodland, keeping left where it forks, and follow this out to the road just left of the junction with Gracious Pond Road.

❻ Cross to a broad track going diagonally left across the common. At a junction by a marker post note the metal gate ahead. The wood beyond is thick with bluebells in the spring. Divert right for 50 yards to find a small path off right and a large pond half-hidden among trees. If time permits walk around the pond and watch the antics of the ducks.

PLACES of INTEREST

Great Cockcrow Railway, Hardwick Lane, Lyne, Chertsey. There's a choice of routes on this miniature railway, complete with signalling system. Shop and refreshments. Open Sunday and bank holiday afternoons from May to October. Telephone enquiries Monday to Friday 01932 255500 and Sunday 01932 565474. Take the A319 Chertsey Road, then the A320 just past St Peter's Hospital. Turn left into Holloway Hill and soon right along Hardwick Lane. **Brooklands Motorsport & Aviation Museum**, open all year Tuesdays to Sundays and bank holidays. On the B374 at Weybridge near the A3 and the M25 junctions 10 or 11. There is always something to see and many special events are staged throughout the year. Ideal for a half-day visit. Telephone: 01932 857381.

❼ Return to the metal gate and, with this on your right, go through a horse barrier onto a footpath with a bank to the right. Watch for a stile on the right at the corner of a field. Cross this, keeping beside a fence then straight ahead to the left of a wood. Following yellow markers, cross another stile and field and join a fenced track. Keep ahead between the buildings of Chobham Park Farm along a lane past houses and through a white painted wooden gate. Just beyond the brick wall right, turn right over a stile onto footpath 52. Pass the gates to Chobham Park House then turn left over a stile to go uphill to another stile. Head for a fingerpost in the corner by trees, cross a stile and walk downhill. Ignore a stile to the right and find a stile in the left-hand corner. Cross this and turn left over a second stile. Follow the field edge round right to a further stile then go down to Mincing Lane.

❽ Turn left to join Chertsey Road, then left again, passing fields and an entrance to Bridgewater Farm left and Oaklands Farm right. Just past this watch for a stile and fingerpost on the right opposite a second entrance to Bridgewater Farm. Over the stile go diagonally left to the top of the field to find a footbridge over a stream, behind a line of oaks. This is the Mill Bourne again. Across the footbridge turn right, keeping beside the stream to walk back through meadows to the village. The tall spire of Chobham church will come into view through the poplar trees as the path finally turns left by garden hedges towards the cricket field and the start of the walk. Turn right on the track beyond the car park to reach the High Street beside Saddlers Halt tearooms. Turn left to the church and the Sun.

The cannon in Chobham village.

LALEHAM

Length: 3½ miles

Getting there: From Chertsey on the B375, turning left immediately after Chertsey Bridge alongside the Thames. From Staines 2 miles south on the B376 (see map).	Parking: Free car park by the river. From Chertsey it's the second car park beyond the campsite. From other directions go down Ferry Lane, opposite the Three Horseshoes (see map).	Maps: OS Landranger 176 West London; Pathfinder 1190 Weybridge, Esher and Hampton Court (GR 051683).

This village has two faces. One is the tranquil Thames-side path and parkland of Laleham Abbey, the other the 12th-century church, attractive houses, pubs and old cottages and the lanes linking the two. The mix of houses and cottages from different periods reminds one that this community was in existence at the time of the Domesday Book.

The walk explores both. It starts beside the river where there is plenty of grassy open space for games and picnicking and even a couple of barbecue sites, so come prepared! The Thames Path is followed to

FOOD and DRINK

The wisteria covered Three Horseshoes pub has many tales to tell. The Prince of Wales was entertained here in the 1920s and Sir Arthur Sullivan once acted as the barman. Today it is still deservedly popular with a restaurant and interesting, carefully prepared bar meals. Try the moussaka with a Greek salad or lasagne al forno and enjoy it either in the intimate 'No Smoking' snug, a quiet corner of the bar or out in the garden. Telephone: 01784 452617.

Penton Hook Lock where the river is crossed to reach Penton Hook Island. Returning alongside the river with its quiet traffic, the route then turns into the narrow Blacksmiths Lane to explore the village before returning through the parkland of Laleham Abbey, now maintained as a public open space.

THE WALK

❶ Start by the information board which identifies the variety of wildfowl frequenting this area, including Arctic migrants. Cross the road to the river and turn right over the grass where swans, ducks and Canada geese strut. Follow the Thames Path sign and enjoy the views along this quiet stretch of the Thames, admiring big clumps of yellow water iris in season. At first the path is a metalled lane where the bankside is cared for as extended garden to the houses. It then becomes a footpath before again being metalled where Blacksmiths Lane joins opposite Harris Boatbuilders Limited. A fingerpost indicates 2¼ miles to Staines.

❷ Continue past Laleham Boatyard on the opposite bank and the Thames Water

station feeding the large Queen Mary reservoir, and reach a weir. Pass beside a white vehicle barrier into the area of Penton Hook Lock, pleasantly laid out with seats where you can watch the cruisers and an occasional barge. The Lock Keepers House bears the date 1814. Cross the footbridges over the lock and then the weir to step off onto Penton Hook Island. The Hook is a dramatic meander and the lock channel creates an island. The salmon ladder at the weir is one of a chain from Teddington to Whitchurch. Paths through light woodland lead to picnic tables at the far end, and a special wetland area. Take some time to explore this delightful, rather secretive place. The lock was dug by hand early in the 19th century and an information board explains the development of the river route hereabouts and the variety of wildlife to be seen. I particularly enjoyed the birdsong and the butterflies and you may see a heron or a kingfisher.

❸ Retrace your steps towards Laleham,

PLACES of INTEREST

The Walled Garden – Sunbury on Thames. This former kitchen garden within Sunbury Park is now formally planted to show styles from different centuries and has several plant collections including a Victorian rose garden. Open from dawn to dusk it is a tranquil spot and easily found on Thames Street beside the river. It is yet another contrast to add to those already encountered on the walk. Admission is free. **JGF Passenger Boats** offer 45 minute river trips from Walton Bridge, easily reached from Laleham on the B376. Open Easter to the end of September. Telephone: 01932 253374.

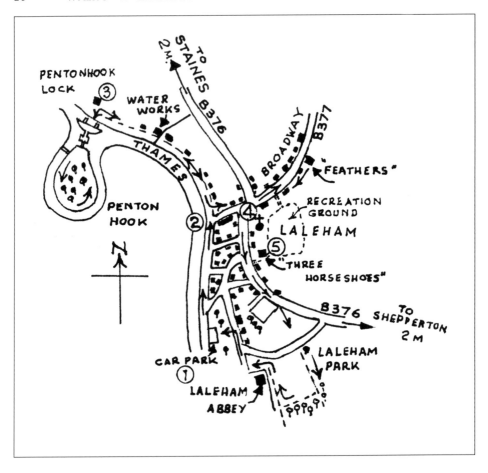

about ¾ mile, to Blacksmiths Lane and a sign 'To the Shops' (map 2). Notice old boundary stones for the City of London at the foot of the walls on either side. Turn left along this quiet lane past a mix of small, mostly brick cottages to reach the main road by a large Regency style house, its balcony draped with wisteria, and opposite the church. A plaque reminds you it has stood here since Norman times although the tower is now Georgian brick. Thomas Arnold, the renowned headmaster of Rugby school, and his poet son

Matthew lived in Laleham and are buried in the churchyard.

❹   To explore The Broadway walk through the churchyard and turn right. The charming early 17th-century Church Farm is on your right while further along Glebe House occupies the site of Thomas Arnold's former home. There are other lovely mellow brick houses to admire so take your time to enjoy this other face of Laleham. Turn back by the Feathers. If you wish you can cut across the playing field,

Penton Hook lock.

entering beyond the allotments, and via a little path in the far corner emerge with the Three Horseshoes a few yards to your right (map 5). Otherwise walk past the church along the Shepperton road, noticing the sundial on the 18th-century Sun Dial House, to the Three Horseshoes.

❺ Laleham Abbey Park is reached by continuing along the main road to a bend and walking beside an old brick wall which encloses Spelthorne Council's plant nursery. At its end turn in right to the Park by a children's playground. Bear left over the grass, cross a small service road and find a horse ride in the trees ahead going to the right near the boundary fence. At the end with an open space left, turn right among the trees to a grassy area alongside the wall of Laleham Abbey House and keep ahead. The huge cedar trees are magnificent and the horse chestnuts in bloom make a wonderful sight. You may just glimpse the early 19th-century house designed by Papworth. At the gates turn right along Abbey Drive to reach the yellow painted Thatched Cottage, also thought to be by Papworth, and here strike left across the grass, by a large cedar tree, back to the river and the car park.

RIPLEY

Length: 4½ or 2 miles

<table>
<tr><td>Getting there: From Guildford 3 miles north-east on the A3 then the B2215.

Parking: Turn off the High</td><td>Street near the pedestrian crossing and opposite Wyllie & Mar furnishers, along a track across the green to a parking area on the left.</td><td>Maps: OS Landrangers 186 Aldershot and Guildford and 187 Dorking, Reigate and Crawley; Pathfinder 1206 Woking and Leatherhead (GR 053571).</td></tr>
</table>

This attractive village, strung out along the old A3 Portsmouth to London coach road, has many interesting buildings and, it is said, the largest green in England. Thanks to the new bypass quieter forms of travel are again more evident. Cyclists have a long association with Ripley, the 22 miles from Hyde Park being a comfortable distance for early clubs to rendezvous at the Anchor. A former resident recalls Duffetts cycle shop in 1918 and next door the barber cum antique dealer who rode a well-polished copper framed tricycle; the rider of a 'penny farthing' is also remembered outside the Talbot although 'it was obsolete then'.

FOOD and DRINK

The Anchor in the High Street began life as a 16th-century almshouse, becoming a pub in 1738. Such names were popular along this route for seafarers travelling to and from Portsmouth. The Dibble family are well remembered for their hospitality to cyclists as recorded in an account hanging in the bar. I am told that around 1910 'the landlord Mr Dibble used to give a puppet show from the bedroom window to children on the way to school but as soon as the school bell rang the window shut and that was the end of the show.' The school was between the church and the present police house. There's still a friendly welcome in this cosy old pub serving a good choice of bar meals. Turn right from the green towards the church. Telephone: 01483 224120.

The National Trust owns the nearby Wey Navigation, opened in 1653 during Cromwell's time, well before the heyday of canal building in the next century. Stretches of canal and 14 locks make the river Wey navigable for 19½ miles from the Thames at Weybridge to Godalming. Cruisers and narrow boats glide by, now sharing the peaceful enjoyment of this area with walkers and riders.

It's a gentle walk across the vast green to a very attractive area by Ockham Mill and along one of the prettiest stretches of towpath between Walsham Gates and Papercourt Lock, passing the much photographed ruins of Newark Priory.

THE WALK

❶ Through the railings opposite the parking bay turn left past a memorial seat to Mrs Jane Murray. Fork left and then right onto the middle path across the green and reach trees on the right before entering woodland. Keep ahead on the

waymarked path, crossing a footbridge over a small stream, and continue on a track between fields to a lane. Turn left to go through the gateway to Ockham Mill (1862) with the mill pond and Millwater House on the right.

❷ Past the mill follow the drive round to the right by a fingerpost and go over a stile by a gate. The lane soon narrows to a path winding between fields and crossing small streams before reaching a footbridge over a quiet stretch of the river Wey and shortly afterwards the canal side. Turn left along the towpath, passing Pyrford Place where you may see white peacocks. The hydrangeas reflected in the water are a lovely sight in summer. Many tales hang round the late 17th-century summer house, sometimes called 'John Donne's cottage', one being that it was a venue for bare knuckle fights at which 'two men

PLACES of INTEREST

Chatley Heath Semaphore Tower has demonstrations and working models of naval communication in the last century between London and Portsmouth. Amazing rooftop views with or without using the telescopes. Entrance from the southbound A3 near the M25 junction, along the turning to Effingham. There's a 20 minute walk from the car park. Open end March to September from 12 noon to 5 pm, weekends and bank holidays. Telephone information line: 01932 862762. Wisley Royal Horticultural Society Gardens and Trial Grounds are always an inspiration. These famous gardens cover 240 acres. Excellent plant centre plus shop, cafe and restaurant. Open Mondays to Saturdays from 10 am to sunset (7 pm summer). Members only on Sundays. North from Ripley 1½ miles on the B2215 and A3 – follow signs. Telephone: 01483 224234.

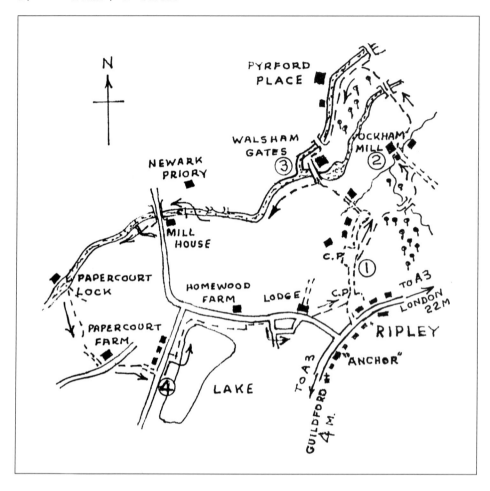

would go in and only one would come out'. The square pond at Walsham Gates, where ducks swim alongside the water lilies, is not a lock but a means of controlling high water levels. Descend the shallow steps for the barge horses and pass in front of the lock keeper's cottage to go left over the weir.

Shorter route: The path ahead leads straight back into Ripley. After crossing a stile and footbridges enter a lane, by houses. Follow this, going right at a finger-post beside Ripley green to the car park (see map).

❸ Turn right beside the river and after passing through a metal gate approach Newark Lock with the ruins of Newark Priory to your right. The towpath crosses to the other side here and comes to a road bridge. Turn left to the attractive Mill House and then right to continue beside the river. Cross the mill stream, go through a metal gate and out across the

Ockham Mill built in 1862.

fields to reach Papercourt Lock and admire the series of waterfalls over the weir. Ignore a stile left and continue to a track by a bridge. Turn left to a gate and stile. Across the stile follow the track over a concrete bridge and further stiles to Papercourt Farm with its curious chimney. Bear right out to a road by a public footpath sign. Turn left to the end of a farm building then go right over a stile with a fingerpost. On reaching a broad track turn right to go over a stile into a road.

❹ Turn left and just past Rose Cottage look for a fingerpost on the right and a path. Follow this footpath to a lake popu-

lar for fishing and boating. Turn left then swing right round the end of the lake and at the next corner look for a narrow opening leading through to a stile and cross this into a field. Keep left and cross a stile to the road almost opposite the entrance to Homewood Farm. Turn right and walk along the road to the impressive gateway to Dunsborough Park. (To avoid the main road, turn right into Georgelands then left along the path to Hedgecroft Cottages and come out opposite the gateway.) Take the path by a fingerpost on the right of the entrance, going behind houses and across the green to the car park.

WALK 5

ESHER – WEST END

Length: 3½ miles

Getting there: From Esher 1 mile south or from Cobham 2 miles north on the A307. Turn down West End Lane opposite the entrance to Claremont Gardens (NT).

Parking: From near the Prince of Wales turn into Winterdown Road beside the green. Either park along here or at the end turn left under a height restriction barrier to a parking area beside the track (1A on map).

Maps: OS Landranger 187 Dorking, Reigate and Crawley; Pathfinder 1190 Weybridge, Esher and Hampton Court (GR 129639).

If a sense of community and a quiet rural setting justify calling this a village then so it is. The large triangular green with its pretty pond is bordered by a row of mainly early Victorian villas and cottages; a mixture of old and new lying harmoniously together. St George's church is a 'tin tabernacle' facing the green. The backdrop is Arbrook, West End, Fairmile and Esher Commons. It is best to look at an OS map to see just how extensive they are. The army used them for training in the last war and the Scots pine provided pit props to help the 1914–1918 war effort. Now much of the area is a Site of Special Scientific Interest (SSSI) and home to the common lizard, heathland butterflies and the green woodpecker.

After a short stretch beside the river Mole, where a resident reports seeing otters in his boyhood, the walk is across the commons to Black Pond. The springs there feed the lake in Claremont Gardens (NT). It's a good walk any time of year and there are seats at several points en route.

THE WALK

❶ From the pond near the Prince of Wales walk up the green beside Winterdown Road and pick up a path at the edge of woodland, still parallel with the road and opposite Garson Farm shop. Cross a railed footbridge and take a clear diagonal path through the trees to reach a broad track and a sign 'Elmbridge Commons' near the parking area at 1A.

❶A Go past a vehicle barrier up a wide gravel track beside a PYO strawberry field with a parallel woodland path on the left. At a marker post keep beside the field fence where it says 'No Horse Riding'. As the ground rises fork right through woods, still skirting the strawberry field. Approach a group of trees and a seat and go forward to glimpse the river Mole down below and views over the river plain beyond. Over to the left of the seat drop down on a path beside a barrier saying 'Footpath Only' to find a flight of steps leading down to the river. At the bottom detour right if you want to explore this corner of the Mole. Otherwise turn left along the river bank until you reach a seat and just beyond it a fingerpost. This is a pretty spot to stop. Watch for bubbles raised perhaps by eels, bream or tench.

❷ Take the path uphill, signed to 'steps and car park'. The halfway seat is a good idea! At the top turn left onto a broad path and shortly turn right, descending slightly and crossing another track. Keep ahead past a white house and arrive at a slightly sunken crossing track under pylons. Here turn right and reach the road by the entrance to The Homewood. Cross the road to a horse ride with white wooden railings. A few yards ahead turn left onto an unsurfaced roadway and almost immediately, in quick succession, fork right and then left on a narrower path left of a sign 'Elmbridge Commons'. Beyond a horse barrier the path broadens out, bordered by pine trees and a ditch, and leads to a junction of paths.

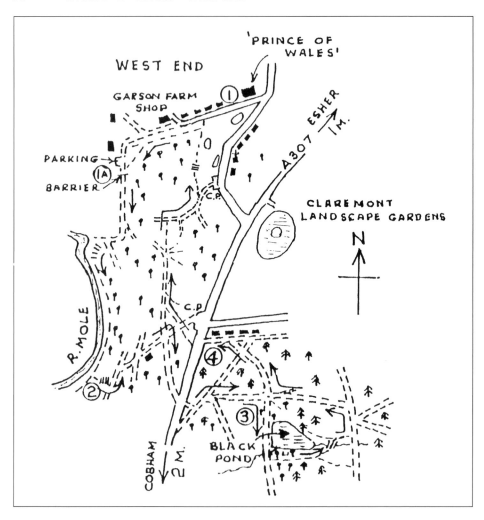

❸ Turn right on a broad path with a marker post and soon a view of Black Pond opens up with seats alongside. At the end of the pond, having gone over a culvert, turn left and pick up a small path through the woods running parallel with the lake and reach an information board which suggests you look out for damsel flies and the common lizard in this area. Shortly beyond this fork left and soon cross a plank bridge.

Bear right onto a crossing path to reach a broad track. Turn left up to a junction of paths with a post for 'Fiveways'. Ignore all turnings to the right and keep round left on a broad path which soon has a series of wooden railings on the left. Go through the first of these where it says 'Footpath Only'. Walk down between Scots pines and then more mixed woodland and, just beyond a small path coming in on the right, arrive

St George's church.

back at the junction of paths at 3 (see map). Turn right along the main track, cross a cleared area under pylons and keep forward through the trees to cross paths and a sign 'Elmbridge Commons'. Continue ahead beside a garden fence to the road.

❹ Cross to the bus stop opposite. Take a sandy path ahead and shortly go over a crossing track, then slightly uphill, keeping round to the right at a T-junction. At a path junction near an open space right, go forward on a 'Horse Ride' with a fingerpost and blue marker. Keep ahead on the ride, ignoring side paths, and arrive in a clearing where six paths converge. Keep ahead on the high ground towards silver birches, ignoring all paths off right and leaving the ride which goes downhill left. Stay on the high ground at first but shortly go forwards downhill to a T-junction and turn right. Follow a well-trodden path over a humpy area with the remains of a brick wall on the right. Bear left at a path junction and at the next crossing path again go left and enter an open area. Almost immediately leave the main path, forking left on a small path through the grass to a horse barrier and fingerpost directing you forward to West End village. Go down a few steps and straight on through woodland on a surfaced path. Just beyond a pond, where I spotted a kingfisher, you arrive back on the village green.

HEADLEY

Length: 5 miles

| Getting there: From Leather-head 2½ miles south-east on the B2033.

Parking: National Trust car park | beside Headley Heath Road opposite the cricket field. Fee for non-members; members display card. | Maps: OS Landranger 187 Dorking, Reigate and Crawley; Pathfinders 1207 Caterham and Epsom Downs and 1206 Woking and Leatherhead. (GR 205539). |

This is a special spot 600 feet high on a narrow chalk ridge of the North Downs but capped with sandy shingle deposits from an age when it is thought the surrounding area was a sea and the higher parts of the downs were a series of islands. So it is a place of contrasts. The National Trust manages 530 acres of Headley Heath, with gorse, heather and birch on the sandy heathland. Not far away a pre-Roman trackway runs along high ground overlooking the weald, which the Romans developed as Stane Street between London and Chichester. Here there is wild thyme underfoot, clematis or old man's beard and other chalk loving plants.

Between the two ridges lies a 'dry valley', with the distinctive steep sides and curving tops of this chalkland feature. The goldeny coloured local flints are used both whole and knapped in the chancel and nave of the church although the tower is of the usual darker kind. The village clusters on the sheltered hillside below the prominent church; a small community dating back to Saxon times, for whom flint quarrying has helped to provide a living.

This rewarding walk, which includes part of Stane Street, is very varied, at first through fields, then woodland and finally across the heath with good views throughout. The contrasting flora of chalkland and sandy heath are easily compared within this short distance and it is probably at its best in spring, summer or autumn.

THE WALK

❶ From the tea caravan walk to the rear of the car park and turn right through a gap in the bank onto a grassy path parallel with the road. In 100 yards fork left and, after crossing a horse ride, reach a small lane. John Wesley preached nearby in 1791. Turn right past Heath House to the road. Cross straight over onto a short stretch of unsurfaced lane, turn right at the end past a pretty cottage, The Heath, and shortly reach another road. Cross carefully, go left a short way then turn

right down a drive. At the end cross a stile onto a footpath between fences. Headley church spire is now in view to the left. Over a stile turn diagonally left, crossing two fields and further stiles to a lane in front of the Old Rectory. The distant roar of the M25 is a reminder that the proposed route was through the village. Cross the stile ahead and continue up to the church over a series of stiles and across a bridle-track. By the lych gate there is a remarkable view north across London. Epsom racecourse and its grandstand are easily spotted. Walk through the church-yard where yew trees outline the site of an earlier church. The little flint building housing a font is the Faithfull family vault, built with rubble from the old church. More easily missed is the sundial over the church porch.

❷ Walk down to the road by the Cock Horse and cross to the right of The Old Schoolhouse. Take the left-hand path skirting the garden and continue between fences to a metal kissing gate. Note the arrows on a marker post and keep left downhill. Go over stiles and between fences to reach another kissing gate leading into a lane. Turn right, passing the Elizabethan Slough Farm, and walk gently

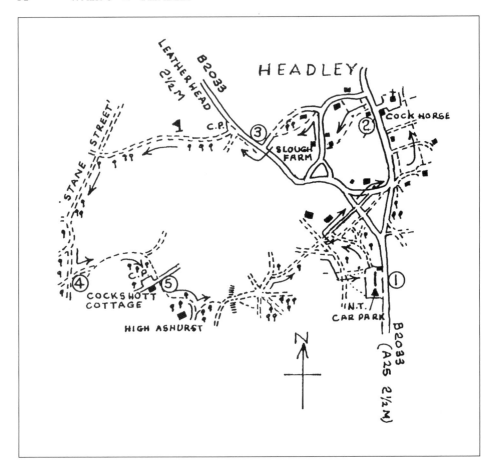

uphill to a junction. Go left into Langley Lane and soon turn left over a stile in front of a very pretty flint cottage. Continue across two fields and over stiles to the top of the rise. The view is impressive towards Box Hill and the dip of the Mole valley. Go slightly right in the next field towards a wood and keeping this on your right reach a stile. Over this turn left along a public byway to the road.

❸ Cross the road and turn right along the horse margin to a small parking area. Take the right-hand bridleway alongside a golf course with extensive views north-west. Later there are views left and Ranmore church spire can be seen on the skyline. Continue for ¾ mile to a junction of tracks and a four-way fingerpost indicating the crossing with the ancient Stane Street. Pause to enjoy the views yet again before turning left, signed to Mickleham. The path goes straight on, as you might expect, mostly through light woodland. Ignore paths off right, the first to Givons Grove, the second to Mickleham where the path dips down and

The Faithfull family vault to be found in the churchyard at Headley.

then rises again, keeping forward on a broad track until you reach a crossing bridleway and a marker post with a purple arrow pointing left and reading 'NT Long Walk'.

❹ Turn left along this path and shortly reach an open area with a crossing track and just ahead another NT Long Walk marker post. This is the top of Mickleham Down. Turn left along the track, bounded on the right by a series of white posts. Where these end and the path becomes enclosed watch for a marker post right with another purple arrow indicating the Long Walk. Take this narrower path going gently downhill at first and then more steeply to a small lane opposite the tiny flint Cockshott Cottage.

❺ Take a bridleway left of the cottage which continues the NT Long Walk, going uphill between fields, then through woodland and finally beside an old wall to a NT 'Headley Heath' sign. To the right is High Ashurst, now a Surrey County Council outdoor centre. Turn left downhill on a broad, stony track. At the bottom turn left and keep ahead to go uphill on a very stony track and reach the junction of six broad paths. Take the second left and soon turn right under trees onto a bridleway with a plain blue marker arrow. Reach a broad crossing track, with a large house over to the left. Turn right, going slightly uphill, and keep ahead as paths merge to a grassy play area on the left and cross this to the car park.

BLETCHINGLEY

Length: 2 miles

STYCHENS LANE

Getting there: From Redhill 3 miles east or from Godstone 1½ miles west on the A25.	Parking: Alongside the High Street.	Maps: OS Landranger 187 Dorking, Reigate and Crawley; Pathfinder 1207 Caterham and Epsom Downs (GR 326507).

The broad High Street rising towards Castle Hill is impressive and lies on the crest of a narrow band of Lower Greensand which expands further west to form the Surrey Hills. It carries the A25 and is bordered by attractive tile-hung houses. The village's distinctive form comes from its origins as an early 13th-century borough, laid out by the de Cleres, a family of Norman barons who used the prominent hill top to site their castle. The lower part of the High Street formed a large market place, readily envisaged if Middle Row is thought of as side-stalls which only later became permanent residences and shops. The Norman church faced it with the main street, now Church Walk, running alongside. Not until 1800 did the road cut through by the Prince Albert. Suddenly, with only a tiny jump of imagination, the scene falls into place; it would still be a good spot today for a market if the A25 were to close! Many houses are much older than they appear, 'modernised' in the 18th and 19th centuries to conceal the timber framing. Altogether it makes an attractive mix and a delight for those who like to spy out architectural detail. For a detailed and beautifully illustrated account the Parish Council publication *Blechingley Village and Parish* by Peter Gray is on sale in the village.

The walk leaves through the churchyard and crosses fields to an old lane leading to the top of Castle Hill where there are quite breathtaking views over peaceful parkland to the folds of the downs. Even the nearby M23 can't take that away. Returning down the High Street there's time to enjoy this most attractive street village and its wealth of old houses.

THE WALK

❶ From the war memorial near the post office go down Church Walk between the pillar box and The Old Butchers Shop. This is the former main street bordered by very pretty and very old cottages. Obberds is thought to be the oldest, its front added, probably as a shop, in the 15th century. The 16th-century Nicholas Woolmers Cottage by the churchyard may well have had shuttered openings under the jetty. Cross the churchyard to the right. The Norman tower remains but the nave and chancel are in the lovely Perpendicular style. Note the 'squint'; Brother Roger occupied a hermit's cell here in 1233. Leave by a gate and steps down to a lane. Turn left, with a view across to the North Downs opening out in front of you, to the old telephone exchange and turn left again by a fingerpost opposite Bletchingley Golf Club entrance, to go alongside the golf course to a three-way fingerpost. Ignoring the stile on the right, go over the grass and bear right downhill alongside a post and rail fence to a stile. Keep ahead across the field to a corner by the bank with the continuously moving silver thread of the M25 to the right in the valley. Keep forward across a stile and go down the side of the next field to a further stile leading onto a surfaced path.

❷ Turn left on an old lane coming up from Brewer Street. After crossing Dormers Farm drive continue up the path ahead, above the lane, to a junction of lanes by a small engineering works. Turn right up steps to a small playing field then left to a path along the top. Turn left and rejoin the lane by Tilburstow House, turning right to meet the A25 beside The Manse, an early style of timber-framed house, dated 1600.

❸ Cross the top of the High Street (the

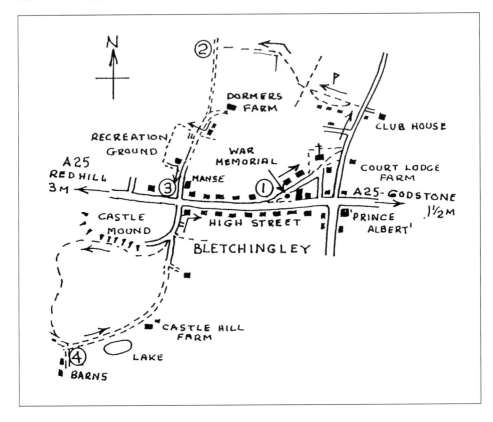

A25) and go down Castle Square. On the left, with seats, is the site of the village pound last used in 1899. At the end where the roadway branches take the footpath straight ahead, signposted as part of the Greensand Way (GW). It's a dramatic little path circling round the mound where the medieval castle once stood. Don't miss a large fallen oak beside the path, cut to provide seating while you pause to absorb the view. The path goes down to a stile and on between fences to another stile near a field gate.

❹   Turn left to the junction of tracks ahead and go left. Reach a stile and gate near an attractive pond used by Foxboro Angling Club and follow the track which curves uphill to another gate and stile beside Castle Hill Farmhouse then continues uphill to return to Castle Square. Walk forward to the High Street, cross over and turn right down to the starting point.

A splendid view across the Weald to the South Downs.

PLACES of INTEREST

Godstone Farm is a children's farm with young animals and 'climb in' pens, all in a lovely setting. Special displays of bee-keeping, spinning and the dairy will interest everyone. An adventure playground, a shop and refreshments make it ideal to complete a family day out (1 adult free with each paying child). Open daily from March to October and at weekends from November to February. Telephone: 01883 742546. From Bletchingley take the A25 east towards Godstone for 2 miles and turn right along Rabies Heath Road. At the end turn left along Tilburstow Hill Road. The farm is on the right on the outskirts of Godstone.

LIMPSFIELD and THE CHART

Length: 6 miles

Getting there: From Godstone (M25 junction 8) 3½ miles east or from Westerham 3 miles west on the A25.	Parking: Limpsfield Common car park (NT) by Limpsfield Chart Golf Club and opposite Grub Street, on the A25 (see map).	Maps: OS Landranger 187 Dorking, Reigate and Crawley; Pathfinder 1208 Sevenoaks and Westerham (GR 412527).

It is not surprising that the gently curving High Street, with houses from the 16th century onwards, has since 1975 been a conservation area. The walk goes the length of it and only a short detour is needed to the church with its very attractive medieval lych gate and ironstone paving. Delius' grave, near an old yew tree, is one of several with musical connections, and an unbeliever lies under the monkey puzzle tree. A church leaflet gives the odd story and other fascinating information. Returning, one sees the picturesque row of old cottages on the corner of Detillens Lane.

This is a good woodland walk, enjoy-

FOOD and DRINK

The Bull, at the bottom of Limpsfield High Street, is a welcoming, comfortable pub with a simple menu of pub food. A drink there on a particularly hot day was life-saving! Telephone: 01883 713402. Joyce's-on-the-Chart is deservedly popular, lovely for morning coffee and teas. Telephone: 01883 722195 for opening times.

---

able in all seasons, across Limpsfield Common and later over The High Chart with glimpses north to the downs. Chart (OE ceart) indicates rough common, important in the husbandry of earlier villagers for fuel, grazing and animal bedding. Its importance today is in affording recreation to those whose living is earned indoors; walking, riding, cricket and golf all take place on the common as will be seen in the course of the walk. There's a lovely open stretch too, passing 16th-century Tenchleys Manor, with amazing views across the weald, this time to the South Downs.

THE WALK

❶ From the car park cross the A25 towards Grub Street and a NT sign 'Limpsfield Common'. Use a NT path with blue marker to walk parallel with Grub Street where the common is used by the golf club. On joining the road turn left on a downhill track, keeping forward past a metal posts to a lane. Turn left and almost immediately right down a small path beside a fence to a stile and houses. Go forward down broad stone steps and turn left along a track to the High Street at Limpsfield beside the Bull. Opposite is Detillens, a medieval hall house with a

Georgian façade. Detour right to visit the parish church.

❷ To continue walk up the High Street. Notice Old Court Cottage, circa 1200, originally the Abbott of Battle's courthouse, and the pretty Forge Cottages and Chapel Cottage. By the telephone kiosk and bus stop near the top take the surfaced path left through a barrier up to the A25. Turn left and cross opposite Pebble Hill Cottage to go down Kent Hatch Road.

❸ Shortly after a road off right take a fingerposted path right in line with the road. The golf course is across the road to your left. Keep ahead, ignoring side paths, going gradually downhill then rising up to meet a road by a turning to Stoneswood Road. Cross this private road and continue forward along the main road. Just past a drive to Links Cottage go left on a footpath with a fingerpost and Greensand Way (GW) marker. After a short stretch of woodland cross a narrow strip of golf course, going slightly left to emerge in Chapel Lane opposite Pains Hill Chapel.

PLACES of INTEREST

Two National Trust properties – **Chartwell**, Winston Churchill's former home with his study and other rooms unaltered, and **Quebec House**, General Wolfe's 17th-century childhood home with exhibits relating to his career – are only 3 miles away on the A25 at Westerham. The house at Chartwell is open from March to November on Saturdays, Sundays and Wednesdays, 11 am to 4.30 pm. See handbook or telephone 01732 866368. Quebec House is open from April to October on Tuesdays, 2 pm to 6 pm. See handbook or telephone 01892 890651.

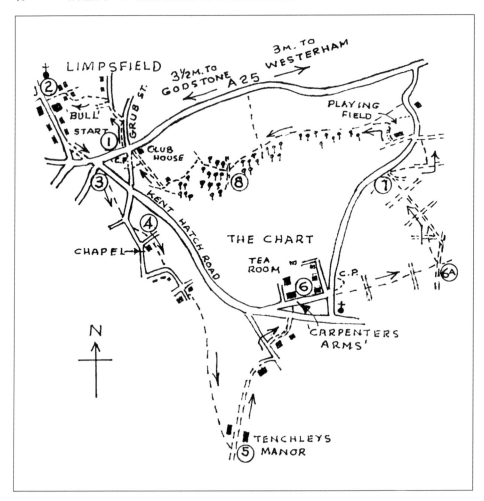

❹ Cross the stile beside the chapel and follow the path into a road beside The Oast Cottage. Turn left on the road and enjoy the spectacular views over the weald. At the end by a four-way fingerpost, take the footpath ahead through a gate marked 'Headland (private drive)'. Just before another gate near the house turn left to a gateway in the fence, following marker arrows. Through the gate turn right downhill on an old sunken track to a stile leading into a field, with views south. Walk down beside the continuation of the old track, towards Tenchleys Manor, once the home of Sir Walter Raleigh's descendants. Go through a gate at the bottom and along the edge of the next field, skirting the farm buildings to reach a track by Tenchleys Manor, of which the tall chimneys are the oldest part. Older still is the trackway, part of a route to Iron Age settlements in the weald.

Limpsfield common.

❺ Turn left, following the track uphill, going through a gate to reach another at the top near a cottage. Stop to enjoy the marvellously wide views towards Ashdown Forest and beyond to the South Downs. Bear right up a drive, past a charming wood carving of a bear and later three cats, and keep ahead to a minor road. Turn left, still uphill, and just past a bungalow take the footpath on the right by a finger-post, following the old stone wall round to the entrance to Quince House. Go ahead up the slope, passing Champions Cottage on the right, to a track ahead which bears right beside the garden of this very pretty old cottage, to a driveway. Turn left out to the road and cross to a path which leads straight to the Carpenters Arms at Limps-field Chart. Joyce's-on-the-Chart is just down the lane ahead.

❻ Facing the Carpenters Arms, turn right to a road junction by The Mill House, the site of a windmill until 1925. Cross over to a fingerpost with a GW sign and follow the path across the common. At a marker post bear left, still following GW signs, and continue on this route bearing right over converging tracks and shortly a broad track. This wooded area is The High Chart and was formerly a deer park. Continue forwards, still following GW markers and later crossing another broad track, to finally reach a junction of five paths and a marker post (6a on map). Here turn sharp left, leaving the Greensand Way, and follow a pleasant heather-lined path round to enjoy clear views of the downs. Meet a broad crossing track and continue on a small path opposite a short way to a T-junction with a broader path. Turn left, going gently downhill, ignoring side paths and crossing a broader track after which the path descends more steeply. Arrive at a junction of paths and a sign for 'High Chart'. Continue forwards to a gate and bridleway sign by the road.

❼ Immediately before the gate turn right on a small path for about 250 yards to a marker post, then turn left up a bank between pine trees and along a small twisting path through woodland to emerge on a large track. Turn left to a road. Cross the car park opposite to the pavilion of the Chart Athletic Football Club and go along the edge of the playing field, passing a seat to the left. Turn left at the corner along a path which bears right downhill to a sunken track at the bottom. Turn left and keep forward to reach a gate. Through the gate continue across a field and re-enter the wood on the far side through another gate. Follow a path along the edge of the wood with fields to the right, past a crossing path, until you reach another gate into a field at the corner of the wood. Through the gate turn slightly left across a short stretch of field to a marker post at the edge of another wood.

❽ Follow a path, uphill at first, through the woods and out to fields. Go ahead towards a stile but without crossing this turn left beside a fence on the right. Cross a stile into woodland and keep forward with fields to the right. Continue alongside the golf course bearing right to reach a junction of six paths. Turn sharp right onto a broad, level track which takes you back to the car park at the start of the walk.

LINGFIELD

Length: 4½ miles

Getting there: From Godstone 4½ miles south on the A22 then 2 miles on the B2029; from East Grinstead 3 miles north on minor roads.	Parking: Car park behind the shops, with a signed entrance in Gun Pit Road off Plaistow Street near The Lockup.	Maps: OS Landranger 187 Dorking, Reigate and Crawley; Pathfinder 1227 Horley (GR 385435).

You may wonder why Lingfield is included; it has almost become a small town since the railway arrived in the 1880s. However, it holds surprises. Once it was two communities clustered around the church and the Gun Pond respectively. The walk starts at the Gun Pond, thought to be the result of removing stone for road mending in the 1600s, while the nearby oak tree and St Peter's Cross, marking manorial boundaries, date from the 15th century. The 'cage' was added in 1773 to contain petty offenders but it has not been used since 1882 when it held a poacher. Roundabout, attractive old houses with roofs of Horsham slabs nestle alongside modern housing. Near the church is a small close, known as Old Town, a real gem with several listed buildings dating from the 16th century, some still used as shops until the 1960s. Church House was once the Old Star Inn and the cottages next to it have their former shop front openings bricked up. Pollard House on the corner is a Wealden style house and the projecting wing was a medieval butcher's shop. You can see where the shutters would have opened down to form the serving counter. The Barn nearby was once the slaughterhouse. A leaflet obtainable locally, *The Village Trail*, has notes on these and other buildings passed on the walk. Just beyond this, out in Church Road, the present Star is interesting too. The roomy and pleasant 1930s mock Tudor, purpose-built pub is typical of its genre. It's built beside a footpath leading from the railway station to the commuters' homes. Just a changing scene with a constant pattern!

The walk is a gentle one, linking several farms on mainly field paths; no hills but several stiles. Quite a contrast to much of the rest of the county.

THE WALK

❶ Leave the car park by a roadway beside the shops. Cross the road by a small round-about to the war memorial and go down steps to walk beside the Gun Pond and see the 'cage' and the old oak tree. Then turn down the other side of the pond on a small pathway into the High Street. A former chapel has been converted to the Lingfield Tandoori, fully licensed and air conditioned; one can imagine what the original worshippers might have thought of such a change. Continue to the traffic lights, and turn left beside old school buildings now used as the Lingfield Day Centre. At the end of the roadway follow a path to the church of St Peter and St Paul and enter the churchyard. Facing it is The College, a lovely early 18th-century house. Go ahead to the gateway at the end of the brick path to find Old Town before returning to the west door of the church. Continue past this, descending a few steps to reach the road beyond the old Guest House, now the library.

❷ Go up steps opposite and along to the recreation ground. Through a kissing gate ahead cross the field to a gap in the hedge and keep forward downhill along the edge of Centenary Fields to a corner where a path joins from the left. Continue down the next field to a kissing gate and into a driveway beside the timber-framed Cold-

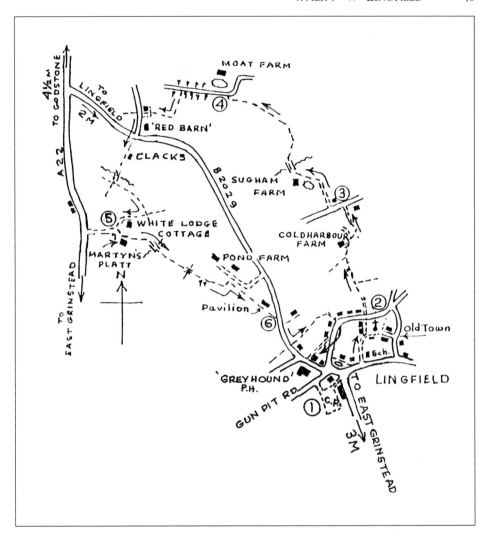

harbour Farm. Soon turn right over a stile and cross a field to another stile, then turn left on a path to Lingfield Common Road.

❸ Turn left a short way, passing the very pretty Providence Cottage, and turn right down a track beside a small electricity sub-station to reach Sugham Farm. Turn right past the duck pond and in front of the farmhouse and buildings to a field gate with a stile. Cross the field diagonally left to a gated bridge over Ray Brook. Keep straight ahead across the next field to a corner by the hedge with a stile and gate-way to the right. Across this turn left alongside the hedge to another stile. Cross the next field, following the direction arrow, to the far corner. Turn left over a

Old Town House, Lingfield churchyard.

stile along a broad track and watch for a small gate with a stone block in the hedge on the right. Cross this into a small lane alongside Moat Farm. Part of the moat still exists and makes a lovely setting for this elegant Georgian house.

❹ Turn left along an avenue of young maples for about 500 yards then go left over a stile in the hedge. Keep ahead to a gateway and cross a stile. Turn right beside the hedge, past a small pond, and continue through a wicket gate along a path beside a garden to a road opposite an equestrian centre. Turn left along the road past the Red Barn pub to a T-junction. Cross the road and go down the signposted track,

passing Clacks with its pretty garden. The path becomes smaller and winds along to a footbridge. Cross this and turn left alongside the stream, soon bearing right beside a hedge and poles for overhead wires. Go past a plank bridge and stile, continuing forward a few yards before bearing right by a marker post towards a brick wall to come out in front of White Lodge Cottage.

❺ Walk forward to join a driveway and keep ahead but soon turn left down a gravel drive and through a gateway beside Martyn's Platt. Follow the garden boundary round to the right to cross a stile by a field gate. Follow the right-hand boundary to go over a footbridge and along the left side of the next field to a stile in the corner. Cross this to a small pond on the right and a fingerpost. Follow the direction indicated across the field, going slightly uphill to the right of a bungalow. Cross a stile and go down beside fir trees to the corner by a gate and stile. Follow footpath signs left over the stile then shortly to a second stile beside the driveway to Pond Farm but do not cross this. Stay in the field, turning right beside the fence to go through a small metal gate. Keep straight ahead across the field (the farm drive veers left), making for a stile and footbridge to the right of the Lingfield Hockey Club. Continue ahead in the next field alongside the hockey ground to the corner, which is rather overgrown, to find a stile leading to the B2029.

❻ Turn right along the pavement, ignoring the first fingerpost left but watching for the next one just before H.Wallis Ltd, garden machinery suppliers, and two timber-framed cottages, one of them thatched. Go left over the stile and along the right-hand field edge to cross a stile in the corner. Bear right across the next field to a kissing gate. Through this turn immediately right over a stile and along a path between a hedge and fence to join a driveway. Keep left ignoring a kissing-gate, and walk out to the road near a bend. Turn right, passing Lingfield primary school and the old telephone exchange and a very pretty row of Victorian villas. Just past the Catholic church and Vicarage Close take a small path right between a holly hedge and a wire fence to the road beside the Old Cage. Turn left passing the Greyhound Inn right and the attractive Rose Cottages left. Continue towards the cage and the pond, noticing the early 17th-century house, Magnus Deo, one of the first in the village to have a brick chimney in the middle, and reach the start of the walk by the shops.

OUTWOOD

Length: 4 miles

Getting there: From the A25 at Bletchingley, 3 miles south on a minor road. From Horley 4 miles north-east via Smallfield on minor roads.

Parking: NT parking area on Outwood Common down the track opposite the windmill.

Maps: OS Landranger 187 Dorking, Reigate and Crawley; Pathfinder 1227 Horley (GR 326455)

A quiet place where country lanes meet on a high open expanse of common, seats are placed invitingly along the edge and guinea fowl strut on the grass. The scene is dominated by the post mill built in 1665 and declared the oldest working mill in England. It stands beside Outwood Lane, a Saxon track running south from the open downs to the Wealden forest, now commuter land. The Bell stands on its margins as an example of early roadside enclosure following the Enclosure Acts. Standing on the green it is easy to imagine how wide it once was.

The NT owns the surrounding Harewoods Estate, an area of farmland and small woods and the walk is partly over this high ground with good views before descending to the flatter farmlands around the tiny village of Horne.

THE WALK

❶ From the car park walk back towards the windmill and ahead down Gayhouse Lane. Just past a bungalow, Knowle Green, turn right down a lane and soon left over a stile. Cross a field towards a wood with good views either side. At the field boundary turn right downhill towards a NT sign beside an entrance to Hornecourt Wood. Continue past this opening, going down the field edge, and in the corner enter the wood, keeping forwards beside a marker post with a plain arrow. The waymarked path descends steadily and at the bottom crosses a footbridge into a field. Keep forwards along the left-hand field edge and crossing over another footbridge to the corner. Here keep ahead across a short stretch of field to the facing hedge and turn left. Keeping this hedge on your right, follow it round a series of corners to walk down the field with Horne church in view ahead left. At the bottom by a marker post turn left and follow the hedge along the field bottom, past field entrances, and round to the left until part way up the other side you find a marker post by a gap in the hedge leading to a footbridge and

another field. Keep along the right-hand boundary to a kissing gate and the road. Turn right into Horne village. The church of St Mary the Virgin sits quietly in its raised churchyard. Its interior is simple but has some interesting features.

❷ Directly opposite Church Farm find a narrow footpath between the former school buildings, now Yew Tree Nursery, and a house, formerly Horne Stores. Clearly Horne is not what it used to be! The school building was donated in 1910 by Alfred Palmer and quaintly has separate entrances for boys and girls. The path soon turns right over a plank bridge and a stile into a field. Turn left alongside the hedge with wide open views to the right. At the corner cross stiles either side of a green lane and continue over stiles along the left-hand edge of the next two fields, ignoring a fenced area and footbridge on the left in the second field. You will begin to see the many pillboxes in this area. Pass a small gate on the left and another pillbox hidden in the trees just before a gateway and stile with arrows indicating a crossing path.

❸ Cross this stile and, keeping round to the left, immediately go through another gate and stile. Initially stay by the left-hand hedge, which is full of sloes in the autumn, and then keep forward across the

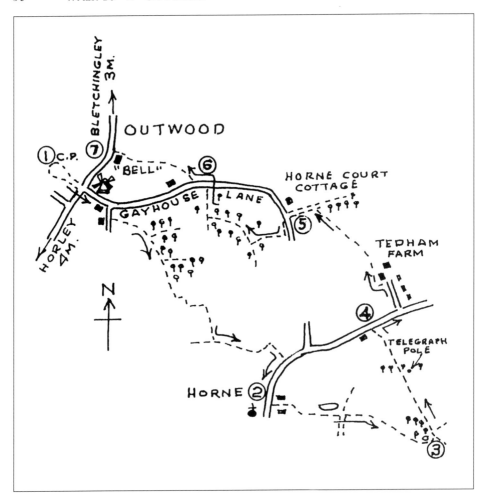

field towards a telegraph pole and go over a stile in the hedge to the left. There are yet more pillboxes in this area. Cross the next field in the same direction to a corner by the end of the hedge and trees and go over the fence by a yellow marker. Cross the corner of the field to a metal gate and a stile into the road.

❹ Turn right and on reaching houses turn left along a drive signed to The Old Cot-

tage and Whitewood Cottages. Opposite a bungalow, Beggars Roost, turn left and soon right beside the garden of Tedham Farm. The path swings left to a plank bridge and stile, then goes straight up the next field. At the top go through the opening to the corner of two fields and diagonally across the left-hand field, pausing to look back at the amazing view. Cross a plank bridge over a ditch and again go diagonally left to a stile leading

Outwood's post mill, said to be the oldest working mill in England.

into woodland. Go past a small pond and over yet another footbridge to a broad track. Turn left on this and come out to the road beside Horne Court Cottage.

❺ Turn left and almost immediately go right over a stile and follow NT permissive path signs left and then right along the field boundary. Turn left over a footbridge with NT markers into woods on a path which runs alongside a bank and ditch to another plank bridge at a T-junction. Turn right, going gently uphill, bearing right at a clearing up to an open field. Turn right on a track along an avenue of oaks to reach a road by a metal gate.

❻ Turn left and almost immediately on the right go over a stile and cross a field diagonally left. You can now see Outwood windmill and there are extensive views northwards. To the left is an attractive 18th-century brick and tile-hung farmhouse. Cross a stile in the hedge and walk down the right-hand side of the next field to a stile leading into the car park of the Bell. Turn right by a public footpath marker into the pleasant garden of the pub.

❼ Cross to the gate in the fence opposite with another footpath marker sign and go left down to the road. Turn left and walk in front of the pub back to the green and the car park.

BROCKHAM

Length: 6¾ miles

Getting there: From Dorking 2 miles east or from Reigate 4 miles west on the A25 then a minor road south for ½ mile.	Parking: Limited parking alongside the green or if you plan to use the pub ask if you can park there.	Maps: OS Landranger 187 Dorking, Reigate and Crawley; Pathfinders 1226 Dorking and 1227 Horley (GR 197496).

Here are all the ingredients of a picturesque village. A well-kept green bordered by pretty houses and cottages, two attractive pubs, the churchyard running along one side and, yes, tucked in the corner the village pump. It's a charming spot and I quite expect to find it on a chocolate box! In another corner there's the pound for cattle and horses found graz-ing on the green, although chickens were permitted to 'de-herbage' it, so it wasn't always such a neat and tidy place.

The walk, however, visits not one but three picturesque villages in this gently undulating countryside of woods and farmlands along the Mole valley, the Holmesdale Vale between the North Downs and the Surrey Hills; very different in character to the scattered and somehow bleaker settlements of the heaths. Betchworth's well-preservied and attractive old houses form a compact grouping centred on the church, which is built in the distinctive light coloured firestone quarried from the chalk downs. The prettiest church is perhaps at Leigh, where Ben Jonson retired. It borders the small green where the old pump is proudly displayed. An attractive old pub, the Plough, and a row of timbered cottages with Horsham slab roofs and old fruit trees in the garden complete the scene. This part of the walk has impressive views.

THE WALK

❶ Leave the green by the Duke's Head down a short lane to the old pound beside the entrance to Brockham Court Farm. Turn left through a gateway on a surfaced path and cross the river Mole. Turn right, going uphill on a broad track to a junction of paths and a four-way fingerpost. Here bear right along a footpath above the river and past houses to continue through fields, crossing stiles and following Greensand Way (GW) signs. Quarry sites on the North Downs are clearly seen. Chalk, lime and hearthstone have been removed between here and Reigate since the 12th century and this only ceased in the 1960s.

Suddenly you are through a gateway and into the attractive churchyard of St Michael's at Betchworth. Take time to look around. Among the charitable bequests of an 18th-century mistress of the former Betchworth Castle is one for 'preferring in marriage such maid servants born in this parish as shall respectfully live seven years in any one service and whose friends are not able to do it.' An ancient oak coffer may have been used to collect the 'Saladin Tithe', ordered by Henry II to finance knights joining the crusades. Offerings are still collected to support missions overseas – same custom but rather different times! Through the lych gate is an attractive group of 17th-century cottages and a long timber barn now converted to a dwelling.

❷ Leave the churchyard through a stone archway and turn right along the road to recross the Mole. The raised footway is a reminder of the ease with which this river floods but normally it's a quiet, dreamy stretch with lilies and dragonflies in their season. Just beyond the bridge turn right over a stile and go straight across a field, skirting scrubland, to cross a stile and ditch. Continue through woodland and

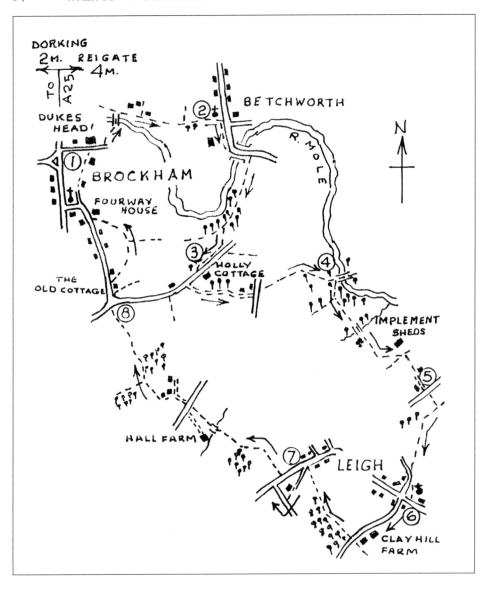

cross a second stile. Walk ahead up the field to a corner by an old field boundary and continue beside the hedge parallel with the lane. Ignore the first stile and cross a second into the lane just past Holly Cottage.

❸ Turn right for 50 yards then go left over a stile by a fingerpost onto a track which swings right then left and leads out to a road past cottages. Cross the stile opposite and go diagonally left to a plank bridge in the corner. Go ahead up the next

St Bartholomew's church at Leigh, with its distinctive porch.

field past stone troughs and a marker post, keeping forward as the ground levels offering wide views. At a fingerpost on the left, by a twin oak tree, cross the next field diagonally to a marker post. Bear left, going downhill through an area of rough grass between trees to cross a stile and continue downhill to the river Mole.

❹ Do not cross the footbridge but turn right by a marker post to go steeply uphill above the river and shortly emerge in a field beside a fingerpost. Turn left beside the hedge and keep forward, crossing diagonally to a stile and footbridge. Cross another field, bearing right towards an oak tree and under overhead wires to a stile in the hedge. Cross the next field diagonally to a corner opposite farm sheds with tiled roofs and go right over a double stile, but first stop and look behind you at the excellent view along the line of the North Downs and ahead to the Surrey Hills. Then with the hedge on your right cross two more fields and keep ahead on a track to a road.

❺ Cross over to a stile and go down a field to cross another stile and plank bridge. Turn right along the field edge to the corner then go diagonally left across the next field to a kissing gate and into a lane near St Bartholomew's church at Leigh. This church is also of white sandstone and its wide porch with Horsham slabs and the square shingled spire make it quite distinctive. Walk through the churchyard, admiring the interesting timbered cottages opposite. Rose bushes will guide you to a gate and fingerpost in the corner leading onto the small green.

❻ Cross the green and go down Clayhill Road beside the old school building. This is one of the links in the 86 mile long circular 'Surrey Cycle Way'. Continue for ¾ mile and just past the entrance to Clayhill Farm turn right by a fingerpost, going up steps and over a stile. Go forward beside the hedge over a small rise, with views of the North Downs ahead, and continue down to a corner where the hedge swings left. Keep forward to the top corner of the field and find a stile leading into a path between trees and wire fencing. Follow this gently downhill and over a stile by a fingerpost into a small lane just before the main road.

❼ Turn left along the lane towards the sports pavilion, beside a children's playground. Walk behind the sports pavilion and, keeping along the back of the field, cross a stile on the far side into a lane. Turn right alongside the cricket ground to a road junction. Turn right and shortly go left over a stile in the hedge. Keep ahead beside a rather depleted line of oaks to cross a plank bridge at the field bottom. Go diagonally left across the next field towards a large oak tree and through a gap

in the hedge. Continue beside the hedge to another plank bridge and stile in the corner and go down between wire fences, turning right over a stout footbridge. Keep ahead past Hall Farm and across a field to the end of an avenue of poplar trees and a minor road. Cross over into the lane opposite and at the first cottage turn left and go round beside a garage to a stile and into a field. Walk beside the hedge to a footbridge and stile at the corner of the fields. Here turn right and walk down, still with the hedge on your right, to the bottom. Go slightly left through an opening in the hedge and continue forwards through the next three fields over stiles and keeping the hedge on your right. Reach the road by the local recycling centre near a road junction.

❽ Cross over and go down the road opposite past Weir Mead Farm. Ignore the first fingerpost on the right and follow one immediately after this, close in the hedge. Go up a gravelled drive between attractive houses which continues as a broad path between hedges. Ignore any turn to the right and follow the main path which later swings left to re-enter Brockham by Fourway House. Turn right along the road where the church spire is clearly in view, passing a small primary school proudly displaying the shields recording the many occasions on which Brockham has won the Best Kept Village competition. Enter the village green by a small path to the right of the church.

OCKLEY

Length: 3¾ miles

Getting there: From Dorking 7 miles south via the A24 and the A29. From Ewhurst 4½ miles east or Capel 2 miles west on the B2126.

Parking: In front of the club house at the end of the green, near the school.

Maps: OS Landranger 187 Dork-ing, Reigate and Crawley; Pathfinders 1226 Dorking and 1246 Horsham and Cranleigh (GR 145399).

Ockley is remarkable for having almost 2½ miles of the Roman Stane Street from Chichester running through it, as straight as a die, carrying the A29. Stretching alongside it for nearly ¾ mile is the broad green, one end of which forms the cricket ground. This is farming country on the gault clay below Leith Hill and the village is very scattered. The old church and Ockley Court are isolated at the north end while the village has developed further south along the street. The Rector in 1872, recognising this, built another church at his own expense 'for the convenience of parishioners'. A case perhaps of 'if you can't beat them, join them'. This

---

FOOD and DRINK

The Cricketers, built around 1450, is a cosy, friendly pub with a separate dining area and a big selection of bar meals, mostly served with chips. Telephone: 01306 627205.

---

church is beside the green, near the school already built in 1841 following a bequest in 1838 by Jane Scott for a well and pump on Ockley Green and a schoolroom. 'The cost whereof far exceeded the sum supposed to have been left; the deficiency being made up by A Benevolent Individual'. Humble too, for the building bears Jane's name. The elaborate shelter for the well now protects a seat. All these changes must have made

quite a difference to the families in the old cottages behind the green.

The walk links six attractive farmhouses on field and woodland paths and passes Vann Lake. This former hammer pond and the woodland surrounding it now form a nature reserve of 8 acres owned by Surrey Wildlife Trust. Throughout the walk views of Leith Hill open up to make a memorable backdrop.

THE WALK

❶ Cross the main road into Friday Street and go gently uphill past houses. At a bend note a crossing footpath but go through a gate with a bridleway sign, past Vann Cottage, and continue along the

An attractive house behind the green at Ockley.

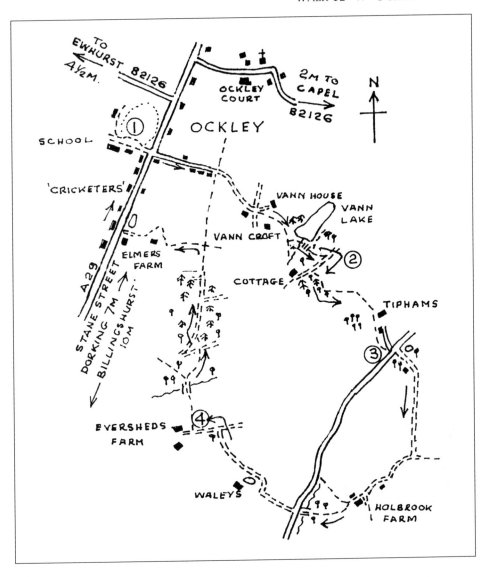

lane where views over the surrounding countryside begin to open up. At the junction with Vann Farm Road go past the gates of Vann House and turn left through a pair of small wrought iron gates onto a fenced bridleway. Follow this round as it skirts the boundaries of Vann Croft right and Vann House left and later goes between fields. On entering woodland turn immediately left onto a footpath and shortly bear right to cross the head of Vann Lake. The banks of trees here are always lovely but especially in autumn. Go over a footbridge and up stone steps, continuing uphill to a track.

❷ Turn right and in about 50 yards turn left onto an easily missed but waymarked footpath, through a small opening by a yellow hydrant sign. Keep forward through woodland, ignoring a path, left, with a footbridge. Pass an old seat made of railway sleepers and bear right along the edge of the wood, using the bank as necessary, with a field on the left. At the corner of the field turn left along the field edge with the boundary trees on your right, cross a stile and keep forward beside a hedge to cross another stile between two metal gates. Go diagonally right towards farm buildings and another stile and gate with a fingerpost. Walk down beside the garden wall of Tiphams and at the corner go left towards a stile and gate and out into a lane.

❸ Cross over to a concrete drive beside a pond. Follow this some way through pleasant open countryside, swinging right and passing a bungalow before arriving at Holbrook Farm. Here turn right down between the farm buildings, still on the concrete roadway. Keep ahead on the bridleway which is now unsurfaced, soon forking left and staying on the higher ground. Follow the track round to the right with open fields left and woodland right. Turn right through a metal gate and descend to woodland. Cross a footbridge and go up to a lane, then up a drive opposite to Waleys. At a gateway turn right and follow the track round beside a fence on the left. Continue some distance between hedgerows and at a little pond on the left among the bushes, come to a T-junction. Turn left towards Eversheds Farm buildings. The farmhouse is a striking building commanding wide views across the surrounding countryside.

❹ Turn right over a stile just before the farm buildings and go down the left-hand side of the field into woodland. Continue downhill and across a substantial footbridge. Take the right-hand path, climbing up through woods to a broader track. Cross this and keep forward through the trees to another track. Keep ahead past marker posts and ignoring turnings left and right. On reaching open fields go through a gate and keep beside the right-hand hedge as far as a stile on the right. Here turn left across the field, over a ditch and up to another stile. Cross this and continue up to the corner of a hedge then turn right, following the hedge round the field. There are splendid views from here, south over the weald and north towards Leith Hill. Keep forward to a track with farm buildings on the left and a duck pond on the right, leading to the A29 road by Elmers Farm, opposite a pair of pretty timber-framed cottages. Turn right along the road, part of Stane Street, using the pavement. Leith Hill can be seen ahead and the Cricketers is soon reached on the left. At the end of a brick wall on the right and Maple Cottage on the left, you reach the start of the walk.

PLACES of INTEREST

Hannah Peschar Sculpture Garden is a dramatic 10 acre semi-tropical water garden forming a 'garden gallery' for contemporary sculpture and ceramics. Don't miss it while you are here; it's only a mile or so away. Go south on the A29 and turn right into Cathill Lane, then left into Standon Lane to 'The Black and White Cottage'. Open May to October, Fridays and Saturdays from 11 am to 6 pm and Sundays from 2 pm to 5 pm. Telephone: 01306 627269.

PEASLAKE
Length: 3½ miles

Getting there: From the A25 between Guildford and Dorking at Gomshall, 2½ miles south via well-signposted minor roads; from the B2127 at the Bulls Head, Ewhurst 2½ miles north	on minor roads. **Parking:** Public car park in Pond Lane behind the Hurtwood Inn on the site of the former village pond.	**Maps:** OS Landranger 187 Dorking, Reigate and Crawley; Pathfinder 1226 Dorking (GR 086448).

Peaslake lies closely enfolded among the Surrey Hills; whichever way you arrive, and I never seem to come the same way twice along the tiny, steep and twisting lanes, you find this little village quite suddenly. It doesn't come altogether as a surprise to learn that it has played its part in the smuggling enterprises between the Channel coast and London. There are myriad tracks over the surrounding heathland with any number of gorse thickets as hiding places, while co-operative villagers would keep their silence for a few marked barrels. Stories are told of farms with back with a fine covering of snow or hard frost. To meet a local husky team racing over the ground is a thrilling experience. The colours are wonderful, the sandy heath is easy going any time of year and the winter trees allow one to enjoy the distant views. A slogan seen on a bus – Get Lost in the Surrey Hills: Find Yourself in Peaslake – says it all.

doors able to take a coach and horse and cottages with unduly large cellars in an isolated part of the county where even early in the last century the Peaslake folk were described as a 'lawless lot' and the 'terror of the people of Ewhurst'.

Nowadays it's a pretty place with many houses built in the local stone and a quiet air of contentment. There's a thriving and well-stocked village stores which serves excellent teas, a butcher's shop and St Mark's church, with a display of Margaret Tarrant's work, half-hidden among the trees on the hillside, while the Hurtwood Inn presides over it all, extending a welcome to the many visitors, especially walkers drawn to this spot. But it's the enclosing and protective slopes of the Hurtwood that one is most aware of: 4,000 acres of carefully managed woodland with public access granted in 1926 for 'air and exercise' and later declared an Area of Outstanding Natural Beauty.

The walk through these lovely mixed woodlands climbs steadily to 857 feet and the site of a hill fort on Holmbury Hill, with exhilarating views to the South Downs and along the line of the Surrey Hills, then makes a gradual descent back to the village. It's glorious on a bright autumn or winter's day and really beautiful

THE WALK

❶ From the car park turn right to the centre of the village and cross in front of the village stores to turn left up Radnor Road by the telephone kiosk. After a few yards turn left by a fingerpost to climb steeply for 50 yards to another lane. Cross and keep ahead down a driveway which becomes a track between fences leading to open woodland. Keep forward and soon go downhill, ignoring paths to either side. At the bottom where the path ahead climbs up, turn right along a very broad track for 50 yards then fork left onto a wide path which climbs gently through lovely woodland of Scots pine and mixed beech and scrub oak, later following an ancient bank on the left. The hillside is covered with hurts (or bilberries) which give the Hurtwood its name. At a crossing track leave

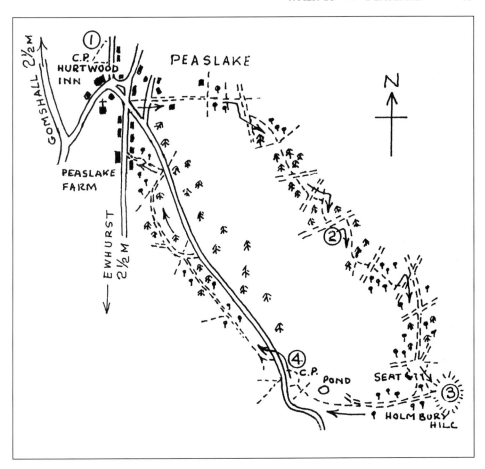

the bank which turns left and go forward, still climbing, to a smaller but distinct path through Scots pines. Pine seeds were introduced to the Hurtwood from east Scotland in 1778 and do well on the light, sandy soil. Improved species have since been planted, particularly after the great storm of 1987, to provide timber. As the ground levels reach a broad estate track and cross this to continue through the trees to another track. Cross this also onto a small path for just a few yards to a junction with another small path. Turn right along this for 150 yards to a wide, well-made estate track.

❷ Turn left and shortly, after 150 yards, turn right onto a clear path into the trees, which meanders gently uphill. As it levels out keep left, past a path going right, to descend more steeply to a valley track. Cross this and climb directly opposite through silver birches and then dip down through a mixture of scrub oak and rowans. Reach a T-junction with a broad track and turn left. After 50 yards turn

A welcome seat at the site of Holmbury hill fort.

right at a crossing track. This wide, heather-bordered track leads across another and climbs gently straight ahead to reach an open area formed by the junction of many paths. A welcoming 'hostellers' seat', with orienteering markers, commemorates the 50th anniversary of the opening of the Holmbury St Mary Youth Hostel. Leaving the seat on your right, take the second path from the right, which leads round left to merge with a bridleway. Keep left and almost immediately the plateau of the hill fort opens out with a circular seat and an illustrated panel of this amazing view.

❸ Return, passing the pyramidal collecting box on your right, onto the path along which you came but now keep ahead on the bridleway, past the path on the right. There is a curved metal seat on the left dedicated to 'All Free Spirits' in memory of two young climbers who died on the Matterhorn in 1987. The view from this spot is superb, right across the weald and the course of the Arun, along the line of Pitch Hill and Winterfold to Hascombe Fort and Blackdown in the distance. Continue by keeping left at a marker post and following Greensand Way (GW) arrows along the ridge with views glimpsed to the left. Go through a horse barrier left, marked 'Footpath Only', and come to an open area with a small pond to the right. Still following GW markers cross straight over a sunken track and keep forwards, crossing another track and a car park to reach a minor road. The view is of Pitch Hill with the Duke of Kent School on its slopes.

❹ From the car park entrance turn right a few yards and then left on a diagonal path through gorse. Turn right on a broad crossing path, parallel to but not in sight of the road. Keep to the main path which merges with a broad, sandy track coming in from the right and bear left onto this, ignoring all side paths including a fork left, to continue gently downhill through pine trees. Just beyond a path coming up from the left reach the road and immediately turn left by a fingerpost onto a footpath going downhill and gradually diverging from the road. Join a track and keep forward to a road opposite Peaslake Farm. Turn right and walk along the wide, grassy verge beside the stream through this peaceful village.

The Hurtwood Inn

WALK 14

SHERE

Length: 2½ miles

Getting there: From Guildford 5 miles east or Dorking 6 miles west, just off the A25.

Parking: Car park behind the village hall by the recreation ground. Entrance along Upper Street beside East Lodge.

Maps: OS Landranger 187 Dorking, Reigate and Crawley; Pathfinder 1226 Dorking (GR 074480).

Cobbett observed 'this pretty valley has a run of water which comes out of the high hills and which, occasionally, spreads into a pond.' The delightfully clear, shallow, fast flowing Tilling Bourne runs through the centre of the village where an old bridge carrying the main street provides broad walls on which to lean, watch the ducks and let the world go by. It's one of a series of villages along this fertile strip between the chalk downs and sandy heathland of the Hurtwood where farming has always been an important occupation but many trades have also flourished in their turn, particularly the cloth and wool industries. Spinning Walk and Rack Close are reminders that Shere was once well known for producing 'fustian', a cotton

FOOD and DRINK

Asters Tea Shop in Middle Street has delicious home-made cakes and also serves light lunches in either the comfortable and attractive tearoom or a pleasant garden at the back (closed Mondays). Telephone: 01483 202445.

The White Horse is a very old building dated around 1475 and has been an inn since the 17th century. Do ask for the leaflet giving something of its history and features to be seen such as the Elizabethan carved chalkstone mantle. The series of small rooms and low, timbered ceilings make this an outstandingly attractive and cosy pub and the imaginative bar meals are very good. Inside there are roaring fires in winter, while in summer you can sit outside facing across the attractive square to the church. Telephone: 01483 202518.

and linen twill. It's still a thriving little place with a variety of small shops and a wealth of interest in the mainly 16th and 17th-century houses.

Many visitors still come to this pretty village, as they have for years, some quite famous, including E.H.Shepherd who is said to have used a clump of pines on Shere Heath as inspiration for a drawing of Winnie the Pooh and his friends. Between the wars it was thronged on Bonfire Night for a fancy dress parade through the streets; one spectator recalls the local Fire Brigade, Boy Scouts and the Dagenham Girl Pipers leading the procession to the bonfire on the recreation ground and that 'the church was always floodlit that night'. The mainly 12th-century St James' church is full of interest so allow time to visit. Several booklets about the village, produced by the Local History Society, are on sale in the church.

This is a pleasantly varied walk, enjoyable at any season, on field paths above

the Tillingbourne valley, then over heathland to Little London before returning through Albury Park.

THE WALK
❶ Leave the car park beside the village hall to come out opposite Lloyds bank. Turn right and then left down Middle Street to the bridge over the Tilling Bourne. Just beyond this turn left to the church with its shingle broach spire, a Norman archway to the south door, an external staircase and a lych gate designed by Sir Edwin Lutyens. Continue past the church to a footpath going uphill through a gate beside the entrance to High House. You soon gain a lovely view of the fields and woods of the Tillingbourne valley. Pass through a small gate and turn right to walk up the field ahead, following a path which bears gently left. Go through another small gate in the corner and continue beside a wire fence to cross a footbridge over the railway and shortly emerge into open fields again. Keep straight on, still slightly uphill, and on reaching a brick wall and a marker post turn right. Follow the wall on the left at first and later go between a hedge and fencing into a drive to reach a road opposite Burrows Lea Farmhouse.

PLACES of INTEREST

Shere Museum, The Malt House, is just up the hill past the Prince of Wales and has a really interesting collection of bygones and items of local history. Open from Easter to the end of September: Sundays and bank holidays, 11 am to 7 pm; weekdays 1 pm to 6 pm; closed Saturdays and Wednesdays. Telephone: 01483 203245.

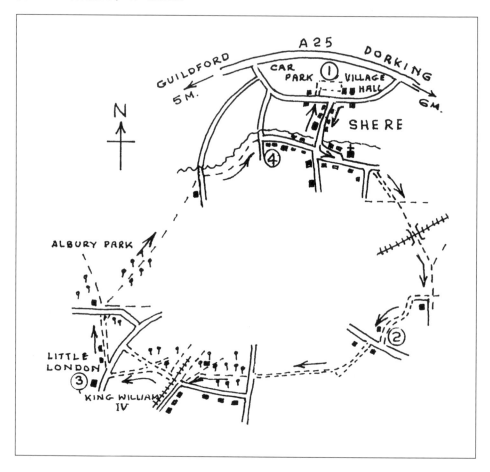

❷ Turn right and shortly left by a foot-path sign down a track between fences with wide open views ahead of you, bear-ing right alongside a garden and continuing through fields with views left across to Winterfold Forest. Reach a road and cross to a path directly opposite through woodland. Keep ahead, ignoring side paths, to join a larger track near a Thames Water Utilities sign, and turn left down to a lane. Turn right, passing Heath Cottage and other houses to reach a white painted gate and go over a level crossing into woodland. Keep ahead, past a path right, to a junction of paths approximately 100 yards before a metal barrier and a road. Turn left on a twisting path with fields to the left and power lines overhead. Reach a road opposite cottages and the William IV pub at Little London, an excellent place to stop and take refresh-ment.

❸ Across the road turn right and fork left uphill on a track past several very pretty cottages. Keep ahead, ignoring all turnings

Looking across the Tillingbourne valley.

right, passing further cottages and houses and reaching a road opposite the South Lodge of Albury Estate. Cross over to where you are confronted with three fingerposts and take the footpath in the middle through a kissing gate. Walk down through Albury Park to another kissing gate and cross a track at the bottom near a pretty fording place on the Tilling Bourne. Keep forward through further kissing gates with the river on your left to a broad track. Turn left and then fork right on a track which reaches the river again and leads out to a junction of lanes near another

ford, with Willow Walk on the right.

❹ Keep forward along a lane with a really exemplary kitchen garden over the wall on the left and pass The Old Prison, a timbered building with flint infilling, and The Old Forge to reach the village centre near the White Horse Inn. The prison was used as such until 1829 and then became a sweet shop until it was made a First Aid Post in World War II. Now it is a private house. Retrace your steps when you are ready, along Middle Street to the car park.

COMPTON

Length: 2¾ miles

Getting there: From Guildford 3 miles south via the A3 and the B3000.	Parking: In the layby outside the village hall, next to the Harrow, or ask permission to use pub car park if you are eating there.	Maps: OS Landranger 186 Aldershot and Guildford; Pathfinder 1225 Farnham and Godalming (GR 956469).

A village community has lived and worked here since Saxon times and probably earlier, at the foot of the narrow chalk ridge forming the Hog's Back. Manorial lands stretch up to the chalk and south to more fertile and wooded country on what is still farmland. The earliest village was centred around the crossroads near The Grange but crept up towards the higher ground of St Nicholas' church in Tudor times, providing an interesting and attractive mix of houses along The Street, dating from the 16th century. The church has some exceptionally interesting features and provides one of Compton's surprises if you have not visited it before.

FOOD and DRINK

The Harrow Inn serves excellent home-cooked food, and the menu always shows originality. Fresh seafood is a speciality. The 16th-century building is comfortable and welcoming with open fires in the winter and there's a separate restaurant area. Telephone: 01483 810379. The Tea Shop, near Watts Gallery, is also a convenient stopping place. Telephone: 01483 811030.

The walk is through the surrounding farmland on good paths with lovely views. A short detour includes Watts Gallery, exhibiting the work of G.F.Watts, a well-known Victorian artist, with a teashop deservedly popular with lovers of home-made cakes. The route then passes the remarkable cemetery and Watts Mortuary Chapel, well worth a visit and best if viewed as another surprise! The hillside was bought by the Parish Council in 1895 to extend the cemetery and Watts and his wife Mary wanted to beautify it. The chapel was designed as a memorial to her husband by Mrs Watts, who trained amateurs from the village to help in its decoration. Returning through the village one can enjoy the old cottages and some very pretty gardens and visit the church, associated with the medieval pilgrim routes which converged on Farnham and continued either over the Hog's Back or via the villages just below it to Guildford. Today the modern North Downs Way passes nearby.

THE WALK

❶ Walk past the Harrow and turn left by a fingerpost down a drive alongside the car park. Continue on a footpath curving left behind gardens. Cross a concrete stile and go up the field by the hedge, past farm buildings on the left and continue down the right-hand edge of the next field. Go over a further stile and straight across the next field to cross another stile by a small protected tree. The large house to the left is Field Place; Felde, a Saxon word meaning a felled area or clearing, was one of the ancient manors and the large fish ponds provided for fasting days. An Elizabethan house with Georgian additions was demolished at the beginning of this century and a 'modern Elizabethan' house built. Loseley House can be seen ahead and left in the distance. Turn right and follow the fence up towards a small wood. Continue around the edge of this field and the next one beside the wood which is full of bluebells in the spring. The view across to the hills is an inspiring one at any time of year.

❷ At the top of the field go through a kissing gate, turn left on a crossing track and follow this around the top of the field, again with woodland on your right. At the corner turn left downhill between a fence and hedge, bearing right at the bottom along a field boundary. Go left at a cross-

PLACES of INTEREST

Loseley House, Gardens and Farm – an imposing Elizabethan house built around 1562 and home of the More-Molyneux family. Open from May to September on Wednesday to Saturday afternoons and bank holidays, it's a lovely place to visit and the shop sells the famous Loseley dairy products, including the superb ice creams. Telephone: 01483 505501. Watts Gallery – open afternoons except Thursday. Telephone: 01483 810235.

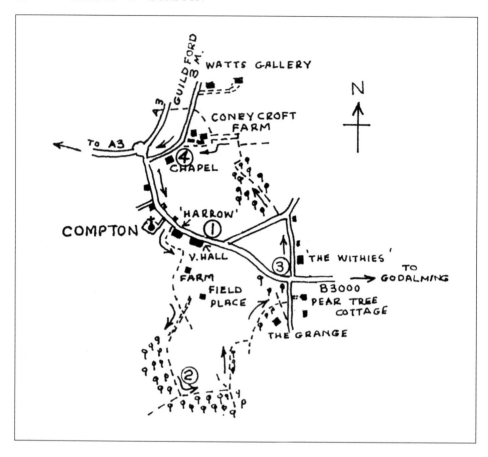

ing track, still with a hedge on your right. Just past a house on the right the path leaves the field side and continues between hedges. At the end turn right and then bear left to a road on the outskirts of Binscombe. The Grange was an early rectory with a fish pond and glebe lands. Turn left along the road, past Pear Tree Cottage, and cross the main road ahead into Withies Lane.

❸ This area is Compton Common and was the focus of the village in the Saxon and Norman periods. Continue along the lane past the Withies Inn, converted at the turn of the century from cottages and a corn store. The owner, Reuben Smith, was renowned for riding a penny-farthing bicycle and wearing a top hat. At a junction of lanes turn left and look for a stile immediately on your right. Cross this onto a well-defined path through woodland. Keep ahead, ignoring a fork right, to a stile and follow the path between the field edge and woods, turning right and then left, to emerge at the end of a concrete farm road just past a stile on the right. Turn left along the concrete road. At the end by the

The Watts Mortuary Chapel.

barn you have a choice.

To walk the short distance to Watts Gallery and the Tea Shop, go over the stile up the slope on your right. Follow the path out to the road and turn right for about 100 yards. To return walk down the road past Coneycroft Farm to rejoin the route at 4 (see map).

To continue the walk, turn left in front of the barn and then right, following yellow arrows and still on the concrete road. Go through a metal gate and turn left towards a second gate and again right and then go ahead over the grass to a fingerpost and a road.

❹ Turn left and shortly reach Watts Chapel. There is a good view over the village from the top of the mound. Continue along the lane and turn left to walk through the village. The path to the church is on the right by the entrance to Eastbury Manor. The mound suggests that it was built on an older pre-Christian burial site and, if so, this explains why it was a little distance from the heart of the early village. Beyond this the black and white, timbered White Hart cottage was an inn until 1780 and opposite was a smithy. Soon after this you arrive back at the Harrow and the start of the walk.

SHAMLEY GREEN

Length: 4 miles

Getting there: From Guildford 3 miles south on the A281 to Bramley, then the B2129 for ½ mile to Wonersh and the B2128 for 1½ miles. From Cranleigh 4 miles north on the B2128.

Parking: Limited parking alongside the green on the roadways.

Maps: OS Landranger 186 Aldershot and Guildford; Pathfinder 1226 Dorking (GR 032438).

In 1892 Shamley Green was described as 'a little hamlet with a collection of old houses and cottages'. That's still a very fair description; it's a quiet place with attractive houses edging an extensive, well-kept green on the flat farmlands of the Wey valley, below the greensand hills of Hurtwood Common and Winterfold Heath.

The houses are mostly 16th or early 17th century, several 'improved' in the 18th century with brick façades. Here, as elsewhere in Surrey, activities other than farming brought a degree of prosperity and tended towards more interesting and well-constructed cottages, enabling them with continuing care to provide homes into the

FOOD and DRINK

The Red Lion, in a row of Victorian cottages beside the green, is a warm, cosy and very friendly pub, deservedly popular for its food. I always choose something different and it's always good. Telephone: 01483 892202.

21st century. For example The Court House, formerly several cottages, is thought to have housed looms for weaving. Nearby Guildford and Godalming were centres of the cloth trade and Wonersh was well known for the blue woad-dyed cloth exported to the Canaries as part of a trade in wine. Aubrey claims this trade dwindled through the fraudulent practice of stretching the cloth but Elizabeth I's taxes on the woad may have helped.

The walk is through attractive farmlands on the slopes of Winterfold Heath to Blackheath, a tiny village in complete contrast to those below. There are some splendid views and it's a particularly fine walk when the heather is out, or later to enjoy the autumn colours.

THE WALK

❶ From the shop and post office go along Woodhill Lane opposite past the duck pond and turn left. Note the tracery on the bargeboards of Barn Cottage on your right. Continue to a footpath on the left going uphill between hedges beside the drive to Sandhurst Hill. At the top cross two stiles and a field to a further pair of stiles. Pause here to admire the view back over the village to the hills behind. Continue alongside a wire fence to the top of the hill and a T-junction with a bridletrack.

Turn right and almost immediately left downhill on a path between wire fences with pretty views over wooded countryside, to a lane beside Blackmoor Lodge.

❷ Turn right past houses, including the most attractive long, timber-framed Haldish Farm, and go uphill towards a gate. Turn left by a fingerpost just before the entrance to Green Lane Farm Estate, and follow a broad path down to Darbyn's Brook. Continue on the drive past the house and round beside the lake, turning right and then left and passing fields with deer, to reach a small road.

❸ Turn right, gently uphill, past Hallam's Farmhouse and about 200 yards further on, at the end of wire fencing, turn right onto a sandy track leading up into the woods. Keep on this sunken sandy track with a blue marker post 'P1' and continue to follow these markers, crossing a gravelled track and ignoring side paths, to keep ahead over Blackheath Common with great tracts of heather seen at their best in August. Reach Blackheath cricket field on the left, set amid the encroaching common, and where P1 veers off to the right, keep forward to a car park.

❹ Turn left down the road to the Villagers and opposite the car park turn left along a fenced footpath. Turn left along a rough track towards the cricket field and then right towards the pavilion. Past the pavilion keep forward with high open heather-clad ground on the left and Scots pines on the right. At a Y-junction among the pine trees fork right and walk slightly downhill to a road.

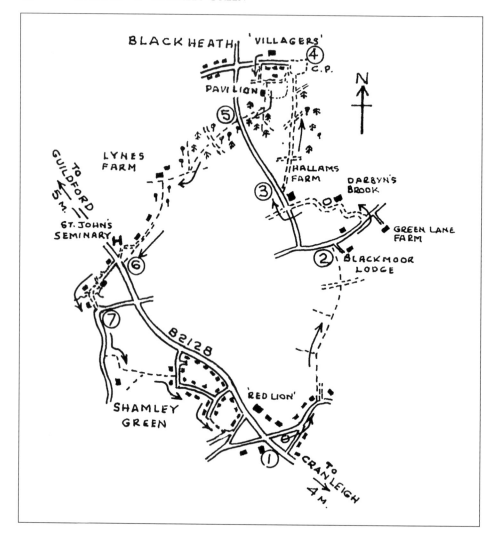

❺ Cross over to follow a bridleway which rises gently through pine trees to a blue marker post '307'. Go over a broader crossing track and continue on 307, now going downhill with blue marker posts to guide you. At the bottom, with fields ahead (confusingly all the marker posts hereabouts suddenly say 307!) turn left and then right, still going downhill quite steadily with a bank and holly bushes forming a field boundary on your right, to Lynes Farm. At a junction of paths beside a farm building turn left onto a narrow path. Reach a gate and continue to a wicket gate, then straight across a paddock to a small wrought iron gate and a stile. Go across the bottom of a garden, through a kissing gate and follow a path beside a

Near Darbyn's Brook.

wire fence and open fields. The path becomes a small roadway in front of houses and where this swings right towards the college, just before the power lines cross the roadway, look for a small, often overgrown path to the left between two metal posts, which goes forward to a road by a kissing gate and fingerpost.

6 Cross the B2128 road to go down a drive almost opposite, marked 'The Mill House'. Follow this, keeping to a wall on the left where the drive divides. By The Mill House Cottage turn left, still following the wall and crossing the sluice from the millpond, past a large dovecot on the right to reach a stile by a gate leading into a lane.

7 Turn right for some way along this quiet, pretty lane and at a bend with a seat go left over a stile by a gate. The path bears right beside a garden and through a metal gate, then left with a tennis court to the right. Cross a stile by a gate and go diagonally across a field to another stile and gate, then left to a further stile and a path out to a housing estate. Turn right uphill and continue to the end of Nursery Hill. Turn right to the end of the cul-de-sac and take a footpath on the left between houses. Where a path joins from the left keep right between a fence and wall to emerge by Sweetwater Cottage and turn left to the village green and the start of the walk.

WALK 17

HASCOMBE

Length: 7 miles

Getting there: From Godalming 3 miles south on the B2130.	Maps: OS Landranger 186 Aldershot and Guildford; Pathfinders 1225 Farnham and	1246 Horsham and Cranleigh (GR 001394).
Parking: Opposite the White Horse beside the B2130.	Godalming, 1226 Dorking, 1245 Haslemere and Hindhead and	

Hascombe is a gem – it is compact, well kept and very pretty. The church, the old school and attractive cottages frame the pond which was restored and landscaped by local effort in the late 1970s. St Peter's church is also special, designed by Woodyer, a Victorian architect, in 1864. It is lavishly decorated and one of the

painted walls shows St Peter and the miraculous draught of fishes.

This is an all year round walk for those who love trees, in one of the loveliest corners of the county. It's Greensand country and the steeply incised valleys give it a special 'hidden' character as at Scotsland, Thorncombe Street or Juniper Valley, while the high points offer superb views. Hydon's Ball at 593 feet is owned by the National Trust, as is Winkworth Arboretum, also included in the walk. Especially good times are May when the famed azalea staircase is at its best or the autumn when the colours are amazing. NT members remember to take your ticket! Non-members can either walk through on the right of way which does not include the staircase, or pay at the kiosk on leaving.

THE WALK

❶ Facing the White Horse turn left along Church Road to discover the pretty village centre. Keep to the roadway round the pond and in front of School House and continue to where it turns sharp left. Keep forward through a gate on a driveway, to go uphill on an old sunken bridleway. Near the top cross a broad drive and soon join another near hay barns, with views over the surrounding wooded hillsides. Turn left along this broad track which, after a sweeping view across the valley left, enters woodland. Ignore a left fork beside a chestnut coppice and continue through Scots pines left and more coppicing right, to a path junction and marker post. Turn left, following a Greensand Way (GW) sign to a T-junction. Turn right, still on

the GW, to go downhill, later swinging left and continuing down to a lane.

❷ Turn right and very shortly left up a grassy bank by a fingerpost and GW marker. Scotsland Farm house and gardens are seen against a magnificent backdrop of trees. Follow the narrow path along a bank and through woodland to emerge in an open field with wide views. Keep forward beside a fence to go slightly downhill and join a drive. Soon leave this as it swings right and keep ahead uphill over the grass (no markers) to another driveway at the top. Cross this, looking for marker posts to the right, leading up the bank opposite and down an open field with marvellous views ahead. At the bottom another GW marker, near a junction of drives, directs you forward along a concrete track. Pass farm buildings right and an oak tree left and follow the now sandy track round a field with woodland on the right, to a stile and gate out to a surfaced track.

❸ Turn left, passing Keepers and continuing past field gates on a narrow, hedged path. At a path junction near a large ash tree turn left through a metal gate, leaving the Greensand Way. Walk straight up a

PLACES of INTEREST

Godalming Museum, near the 'Pepperpot' in the High Street, has a room devoted to the life and work of Gertrude Jekyll, the well-known gardener, who lived at nearby Munstead. Many examples of Lutyens' work, the famous architect with whom she often collaborated, are also in the vicinity. For the museum's opening times telephone 01483 426510.

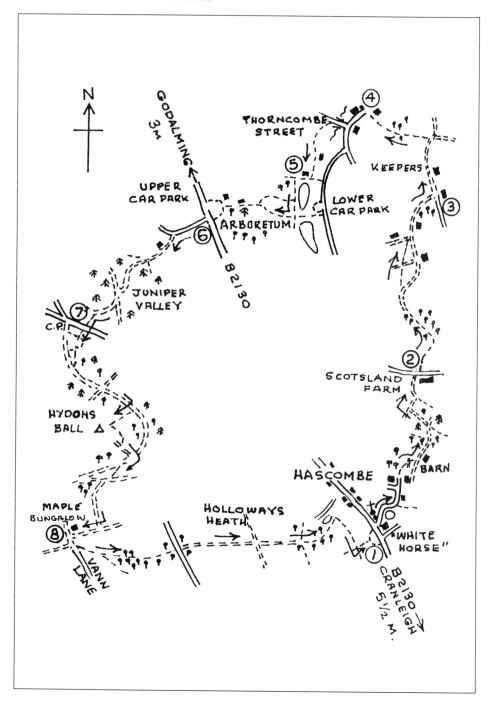

The village pond and church at Hascombe.

field towards woods, enjoying the views opening up behind you over Bramley to Winterfold and Pitch Hill. A small path twists uphill through woodland beside trees planted after the 1987 storm and near the top goes beside a line of sweet chestnuts to a stile leading into an open field. Keep forward beside a holly hedge over one of the highest points in the walk with views in all directions. To the left is Hascombe Hill with an Iron Age fort and once part of the signalling chain between the Admiralty and Portsmouth's Navy base. Cross a stile and go steeply downhill, keeping to the right to pick up a path through the trees, with a second stile part way down the field. Emerge in the lane at

Thorncombe Street beside a timbered cottage.

❹ Turn left past the telephone box and hall to a road junction and then right towards Godalming. Just after the bridge over the stream turn left up a track with a fingerpost to a gateway and stile. Over the stile bear left along the field edge to another stile. Follow the path to a further stile and along the edge of two more open fields, passing a converted barn on the left. The next stile leads alongside a garden and down steps into a drive.

❺ Non NT members not wishing to pay the entrance fee to the arboretum should turn left down the drive, then right along the road to a NT car park. Just beyond this cross a stile on the right into the arboretum and follow yellow waymark signs (mostly pointing the other way) going beside the lake and then uphill to the Upper Car Park.

NT members with cards and those willing to pay can turn right up the drive and, just beyond a stile on the right, turn in left by a NT board, following a path through the woods beside the lake. The sharp eyed may notice the bark split by a lightning strike on one of the oaks bordering the path. Keep forward on a broader track to a path junction by a second lake with a boat house opposite. Here you may either continue to explore the arboretum or, for a more direct route, turn right up the azalea staircase, bearing right at the top, still uphill, onto a broad track which leads past the toilets, kiosk and shop to the Upper Car Park. Cross this to a fingerpost by the B2130 road.

❻ Go down the lane opposite. At the end turn left, signed to South Munstead Farm and continue downhill on a rough track, following it round some way to descend into Juniper Valley. Turn left on the broad track running along the bottom and shortly, at a junction of tracks, bear right uphill. As the track nears the road and begins to level out look for a stile on the left out to the road.

❼ Cross over to a small path leading into a car park and cross this to one of the small paths opposite leading into a much broader track. Turn left, going uphill towards Hydon's Ball, a local view point. Where the track levels out turn right up a

path barred by tree stumps, to reach the top. A stone seat commemorates Octavia Hill, a co-founder of the National Trust, in whose memory the land was donated. A perfect spot to rest and enjoy views across the weald to the South Downs and nearer the unmistakable scarp of Blackdown. Walk from the seat to the trig point and turn sharp left downhill on a fairly broad path. At a T-junction with a barrier to the right go left, still downhill, to a broad track by a NT sign. Turn right and almost immediately left onto a narrow path with a blue bridleway marker to another broad path. Turn right and straightaway left on a path between a field and woodland. Turn right at a T-junction to reach Maple Bungalow near a junction of paths.

❽ Turn left into a small lane and within a few yards turn left again by a fingerpost, onto a small path up the bankside. As it begins to go downhill fork left on the higher path along the top of the hanger. On leaving the woods the path continues in the same direction along the edge of two fields before re-entering woodland to go quite steeply down to a lane. Cross straight over to follow a path uphill onto Holloways Heath. Keep forward, ignoring side paths, across an area devastated overnight in the storm of 1987 and now largely bare of trees. At a very broad crossing track keep ahead until you reach a path (GW) going off right. Ignore this and continue downhill to where the path swings right with a pond on the left. Keep forward through a small gate onto a fenced path. The White Horse pub is soon in view. Go over a stile on the left and across the final field to a stile by a gateway.

CHIDDINGFOLD

Length: 6 miles

Getting there: From the A3 at Milford 5 miles on the A283, signed to Petworth.	Parking: Roadside parking between the green and shops.	Maps: OS Landranger 186 Aldershot and Guildford; Pathfinder 1245 Haslemere and Hindhead (GR 961354).

This lovely Wealden village on the Surrey/Sussex borders can trace its history from the Iron Age yet is still very much alive today. Old houses and cottages with mellow brickwork, half-timbering and the tile-cladding typical of the weald border the green which slopes gently down to St Mary's church and the 14th-century Crown Inn, reputedly the oldest licensed house in Surrey, where both Edward VI and Elizabeth I stayed. The spreading bracket of a corner post is carved from a solid tree placed upside down to suit the purpose. There is a working smithy on the green and nearby a hawthorn tree recorded as a landmark in Henry VII's time, 500 years ago. Some say it is the planted staff of Joseph of Arimathea, others merely the oldest hawthorn in the country! Chiddingfold's greatest fame is as the earliest centre for glassmaking, first recorded here in 1226 and continued into the 17th century. The high quality glass was used in Westminster Abbey and St George's Chapel, Windsor. Higher profits were to be made, however, from the many iron works which flourished between 1580 and 1665. More recently walking sticks have been the local industry.

This is a good summer or spring walk to enjoy the flowers in the fields and hedgerows. It leaves the village through the churchyard then climbs to Balls Down for beautiful views across to Blackdown, following pretty field and woodland paths to the hammer ponds at Imbham's Farm and returning down a quiet country lane, part of the Priest's Path to Haslemere when it was a mere hamlet.

THE WALK

❶ Enter the churchyard, already in existence in 1220, by the lych gate and notice the high coffin rest. The path leads to a gate through a springtime carpet of wild crocus and you may hear the jackdaws in the tower. Through the gate turn left to go through a kissing gate and uphill past trees

to another kissing gate. Keep ahead along a residential road until it turns right, then continue forward between chestnut fencing to a double stile leading onto Balls Down.

❷ Stay along the top of the field, past a stile on the right, and where the hedge turns right cross diagonally right to the corner. There are good views across to Blackdown on this stretch. A stile and kissing gate lead past a house, left, and just before a driveway the path swings right, then left in front of a modern house. Go over a stile into a field and forward to the hedge, bearing left alongside it to cross a stile into a narrow lane.

❸ Turn right and just past Langhurst Manor entrance turn left along a footpath leading to open fields. Go straight ahead to reach a hedge and cross stiles either side of a sunken track. Continue across two

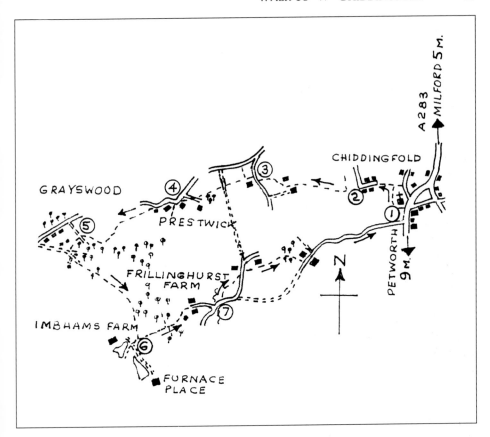

fields with gates and stiles to enter a field with a hedge and a wood on your left. Stay beside the hedge and using further stiles cross a drive and proceed diagonally, with a lodge on your right, out to a road.

❹   Turn left, continuing past farm entrances where the road turns sharply right then left. Immediately after this, by Damson Cottage, go left over a stile with a fingerpost, along a fenced path and cross two stiles to skirt the end of a garden. The paths here are indistinct but with the house behind you, ignore a stile, left, to open fields and go forward below a bank

through light woodland to a field gate. Follow a hedge on the left, enjoying the views across to Gibbet Hill, and crossing another field to go through a gate and reach the highest point of the walk with the land falling away in front of you. A wonderful spot! With a gate on your right go through the one immediately ahead and descend beside a hedge on the right to a gate and stile at the bottom. Turn right alongside a hedge to a stile on the left and cross this into a broad woodland track.

❺   Cross this to a stile and continue ahead along a fenced path to reach a small

Imbhams Farm.

lane. Turn left and continue bearing left past a farm entrance to a gate at the end. Cross the field ahead with a fence on your left, to pass through a screen of trees. Cross two further fields to where a fingerpost indicates a path goes off left at a gateway. Note this path but detour right through the gateway to the pond at Imbhams Farm. Wander left at this pretty spot and reflect that when the Quennell family owned the Imbhams furnace they supplied 'gunns and shott' for Charles I until the Roundheads destroyed their forge. The hammer ponds and 'bayes' hereabouts supplied water power to operate the bellows and hammers and later drive the blast-furnaces used in iron-founding, while the trees were fuel for the furnaces. Earlier still the area was busy with glass furnaces. It's much more peaceful now.

❻ Join the Priest's Path from Haslemere by retracing your steps to the gateway and continuing forward along the path you noted earlier with a hedge on your right. Go through a gate ahead into Frillinghurst Wood. Where the hedgerow swings right, fork left onto a tiny path across an open area especially good for butterflies, where the violets and other woodland flowers are a joy. The path winds through the trees, crossing a stream via a footbridge. After a short rise pass a path going uphill left and keep forward to cross a stile into fields with Frillinghurst Farm ahead. Use further stiles to go diagonally across two fields to a concrete farm road. Turn right and walk down between buildings to a minor road. There was another medieval furnace near the bridge.

❼ Bear left, passing Dell Farm, and as the road rises leave the Priest's Path and find a footpath going up the bank on the left by a fingerpost. Cross a stile into a field and turn half right to cross another stile which becomes visible over the rise. Continue towards a house and a stile in the hedge on the right leading to a road. Cross to a stile opposite and keep forward and, with a house and garden to your left, follow the hedge down to go left over a stile into a wood. Turn right and follow a track to a garden gate marked 'Private'. Here turn right to cross a stile into a field. Turn left, crossing further stiles to reach a lane. Turn left and follow what is again part of the Priest's Path between Chiddingfold and Haslemere, for about ½ mile back to the village at the main road near the Swan pub. Cross and go up the alleyway beside the butcher's shop, below the canted wall of the Crown, to reach the starting point.

THURSLEY

Length: 3½ miles

Getting there: From Guildford 9 miles south or from Hindhead 4 miles north on the A3 then the slip road signed 'Thursley'.

Parking: Limited parking at the edge of the recreation ground or on weekdays near the church (start at 2 - see map). If you are visiting the Three Horseshoes you may ask to park there.

Maps: OS Landranger 186 Aldershot and Guildford; Pathfinders 1245 Haslemere and Hindhead and 1225 Farnham and Godalming (GR 902397).

Thursley, on the slopes below Hindhead, is set in an almost continuous expanse of lowland heath and woodland encompassing great commons such as Frensham, Hindhead, Crooksbury and Elstead, sometimes called 'Surrey's Last Wilderness'. Much of this is owned by the National Trust, including 1,000 acres around Hindhead, while the army owns large tracts to the north-west. Thursley Common is managed by English Nature as a National Nature Reserve. It may look like moorland but supports a very different and highly specialised wildlife and is now rare

FOOD and DRINK

The Three Horseshoes is a well-kept, cosy pub that serves excellent food and good beer. From the garden you can enjoy lovely views across to Hindhead and Gibbet Hill. Open for lunch from 12 noon to 2 pm every day and supper from 7 pm to 9 pm Tuesday to Saturday. Telephone: 01252 703268.

throughout Europe. Around the village, however, is a thin strip of agricultural land running westwards which has been worked since Saxon times and, as elsewhere, iron-founding and glass works have also provided a livelihood. Lying on the London-Portsmouth route it has also sheltered travellers and the old coach road over Hindhead can still be followed. There are tales of smuggling and secret passages, highwaymen and footpads, and a memorial stone in the churchyard relates the story of an ill-fated sailor travelling this road. Cobbett arrived by the turnpike road from Guildford and deplored the broadcast sowing of turnip seed rather than his advocated method in quickly and easily hoed rows, complaining of 'hoe, hoe, muddle, muddle and such a looking up to Hindhead to see when it is going to be fine.' The latter practice certainly continues but now it is a place of ordered tranquillity with the A3 speeding by some way off. This is where the architect Edwin Lutyens was brought up and closely studied the buildings of the district. He designed Prospect Cottage, along The Street, as the Thursley Institute, and undertook the conversion of a pair of cottages and a shop into a house. Both are seen on the walk. It's a rather spread out

village and the walk passes attractive houses and cottages in a lovely setting and goes through the churchyard. Do visit the church with its huge font and beamed ceiling. The route is then very varied, through fields and over army lands with some of the best stretches of heather in the district, returning across the nature reserve. You'll enjoy it any time of year but just keep an eye towards Hindhead!

THE WALK

❶ From the triangular grassy area with the Thursley or 'Thors-Lee' village sign go along The Street, passing Street House where Lutyens grew up, on your right. Turn right at the end into Highfield Lane and walk up to the churchyard entrance with Hill Farm directly ahead. Notice the sundial clock on the shingled tower. 'Hora pars vitae' means 'an hour is a part of life'.

❷ Cross a stone stile by a fingerpost into the churchyard and follow the path round to the left. You can see from here how a fashionable Georgian façade was added to a much older house at Hill Farm. It's a lovely view ahead over a field belonging to the National Trust. Note the large memor-

PLACES of INTEREST

The Moat and Thursley Nature Reserve, along the road towards Elstead. An area of mire or bog with plank walks enabling visitors to appreciate this very special habitat, with insect eating sundews and 20 varieties of dragonfly. Lutyens Car Trail – Waverley Borough Council has published a handbook with a map and car route to help locate a large number of his designs in the neighbourhood. The museum in Godalming High Street has copies. Telephone: 01483 426510.

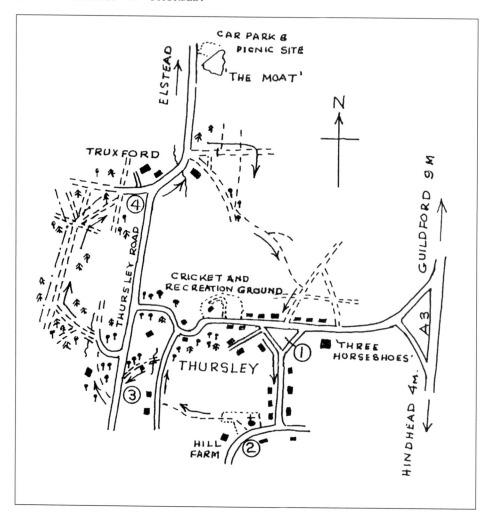

ial stone to 'a generous but unfortunate sailor'. It tells the story of his murder by three villains in 1786 at Hindhead, and was erected by the villagers out of sympathy for the victim of this 'barbrous murder'. The murderers were hanged on Gibbet Hill at Hindhead. Keep left by a fingerpost out to a fenced path, crossing three stiles and then an open field to a further stile leading down into a lane. Turn right past Smallbrook Farm and continue to a fingerpost on the left and cross a stile. Go over a plank bridge, then uphill beside a post and rail fence. Cross another stile by a gate and continue uphill on an attractive, slightly sunken path in an area of wooded parkland. Cross a small footbridge and continue beside a fence and large chestnut trees to reach Thursley Road.

❸ Turn left and over the brow of the hill turn right by a fingerpost. Follow a bridle-way down to a house and go forward over a bridge and straight ahead up a track marked 'Military Vehicles Only'. Keep right at a fork and stay right on the broad track to a T-junction under a row of pylons. Turn right on another broad track alongside the pylons and out to an area of open, sandy heathland. There are a number of tracks on this MOD land but keep forward using the pylons to guide you. At a very broad cross-ing path and junction of six tracks note a larger pylon where the cables diverge into two lines. Follow a path going diagonally right and slightly downhill close to the right-hand branch of the power lines. Reach a graded track and turn left along to cross-tracks opposite an MOD board for The Surrey Common Lands. Turn right down a small roadway to the Thursley-Elstead road beside Truxford Cottage.

❹ Cross the road, turn left and just past a stream turn right into a track by a bridle-way sign. At the fork branch left to a gate with a notice 'English Nature – National Nature Reserve' near a stone cairn with a map of the reserve and an information board on the flora and fauna. Within a short distance, at the second marker post on the left with blue arrows, turn right slightly uphill to a junction of tracks in the trees. Here keep left and go uphill through a horse barrier. As you climb uphill there are impressive views behind you over heathland towards Farnham and the ridge of the Hog's Back on the skyline carrying the route of the North Downs Way. As the ground levels out you can spy Thursley church spire ahead, and left the spires of Charterhouse School on the skyline above Godalming. Keep forward on this small path, ignoring a turn to the left. Further on you may glimpse the Three Horseshoes pub to the right across the gorse before reaching a horse barrier and a broad, sandy track. Turn right down to a crossing sandy track and keep ahead with a field on the left to reach the road at the start of the walk. To the left is the Three Horseshoes pub and to the right Lutyen's first executed work, The Corner. You can see the wing he added at the rear.

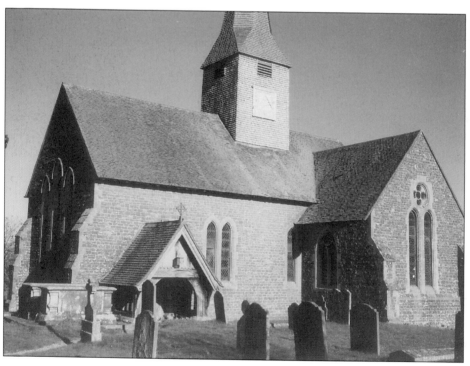

The church of St Michael and All Angels.

TILFORD

Length: 6¼ miles

Getting there: From Farnham station 2½ miles on a minor signposted road; from Hindhead 5 miles on a minor signposted road off the A287 ¼ mile north of Hindhead.	Parking: Either beside the green near the river or use the car park on the left of the Hindhead road, just past the church, and start at 2 (see map).	Maps: OS Landranger 186 Aldershot and Guildford; Pathfinder 1225 Farnham and Godalming (GR 874434).

Tilford can justify the description 'idyllic'. Three small roads converge on the triangular green and two arrive over medieval bridges, for here is the confluence of streams draining the Hampshire hills and forming this upper stretch of the river Wey. The wide, shallow river runs along one side of the sloping green while the Barley Mow and other attractive 17th

and 18th-century houses and cottages are settled along another border. I stood one summer and watched the harvesting, whilst a rider waited as her horse drank from the river and a child paddled. On many summer weekends the pub is part of the cricket scene as batsmen, locals and visitors bring their drinks outside to watch the game, perhaps from the shade of one of

Tilford's oaks. The famous one is the King's Oak, also referred to as Novell's or Cobbett's oak. Novell was a local resident who apparently liked this spot to 'hold forth' while William Cobbett, who was brought up at Farnham, mentions it in his *Rural Rides*. He recalls as a boy seeing a young tree which by 1822 was 'by far the finest tree I ever saw'. A charter of King John refers to the King's Oak here, giving rise to the alternative name. Clearly notable oaks have been on this green for many centuries as they are today. It's a fertile area, farmed since Saxon times, and earlier this century had many hop gardens.

This easy going walk follows the river at the edge of Hankley Common and continues to the larger village of Elstead along a quiet and pretty lane. Elstead has an active village life and many old buildings. It was once part of a thriving wool trade but also noted for growing large quantities of carrots. Leaving Elstead, the route crosses the third of five medieval bridges on this part of the Wey, thought to have been built by Cistercian monks from nearby Waverley Abbey, probably around 1233 after notorious floods. All along the route are pillboxes, part of 'the last line of defence' against invasion in World War II, stretching from Kent to Bristol, and encountered on other walks in this book. The final stretches are through varied countryside of fields and

woodland. If you find yourself humming hymns it may be the influence of Isaac Watts who lived at Tilford and wrote many hymns including *Oh God, our help in ages past*, or A.M.Toplady who lived at Farnham and, it is said, wrote *Rock of Ages* while staying at Tilford House.

THE WALK

❶ Walk up over the grass to the apex of the village green with the Barley Mow behind you and follow a horse ride on the left, 'Mollie's Ride', alongside the road. (This is locked 1st–31st January – use roadside pavement.) Pass the church which has a memorial to a local heroine, Diana Hope Rowden, a captured WAAF executed in a Nazi concentration camp. At the end turn left along a broad track with a parking area on your right.

❷ Follow this leafy walk for about ⅓ mile and reach Stockbridge Pond, also called Abbotts Pond, on your right. A pretty spot and a favourite with anglers. Ice was cut here for the two ice houses in the village.

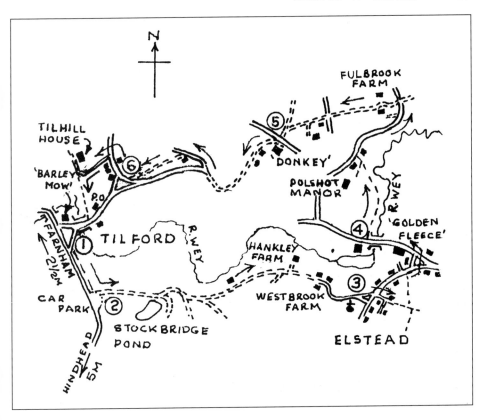

Continue ahead and at a fork go left and shortly after still keep left at a clearing. Continue on the broad, sandy bridleway through woodland of birch and pine, ignoring all tracks off right and following bridleway signs. The river has undercut the sandstone forming minor cliffs and the water meadows are below on the left through the trees. Yagden Hill is over to the right and is army training ground. Cross under power lines and continue some way, passing Upper Hankley Cottage and later a clearing used for parking by the drive to Hankley Farm, until the track eventually joins a metalled lane by some gateposts. Turn left along this quiet lane, passing attractive cottages and farm buildings. Note the stone cladding on a barn near Westbrook Farm. As the road bends around you glimpse the spire of Elstead church ahead. Pass houses and an interesting row of cottages built of the local ironstone, and come to the church of St James on the right with a beautifully carved wooden porch.

❸ From the church take the left fork out to Thursley Road. (To make a short cut turn left along the main road to Hope Street on the left.) Cross and walk up West Hill opposite to the end of the cul-de-sac. Take the footpath which climbs the short way to the top and a stile on the left, just before a path junction from where there are good views. Go left over the stile and cross a field beside a bank. Cross another stile onto a path leading down between fences and gardens to the road opposite the old tile-hung Apple Tree Cottage and cross to Hope Street. Turn right past the shops to the Old Forge. Note the gun placements in the garden wall of the house across the road. Turn left past the Golden Fleece and cross the old bridge over the river Wey, recently repaired and strengthened. The Old Mill produced worsted and later gold braid for army uniforms and Cromwell's troops were billeted in an earlier building.

❹ Turn right immediately over the bridge along a path beside the river and follow this across fields to where it goes between a garden and barns with a path joining from the left. Cross another stile and continue to a road. Turn right and walk with care along the road using the verge and come first to the gates of Fulbrook House, designed by Lutyens with a garden laid out by Gertrude Jekyll, and just beyond to the entrance of Fulbrook Farm. Turn left onto a bridleway beside the entrance to the farm and follow this old track which makes a delightfully shady walk with views across the fields on either side. Watch out for another pillbox disguised as a cattle shed. Reach a road and cross straight over up the drive of Amina Heights to a set of imposing gates. Here turn right up a driveway and where this turns left keep ahead on a sandy track leading down beside small power lines. At the bottom turn left to the road.

❺ Cross over and turn right down the drive to the Donkey public house. Walk past the pub and the entrance to Pound House and at a junction of driveways turn left past the entrance to Ravenswing. Keep ahead on the track and after about ½ mile reach Whitmead and the elbow of a small road. Turn right, going quite steeply uphill to reach a letterbox and Highmead on the right and Pooh Corner on the left. Turn left down the footpath beside Pooh Corner, going through woodland and continuing on a smaller path between fences with fields either side. Reach the entrance to Archers Hill and keep ahead down the drive past Tile House. At a T-junction take the right-hand fork out to the main road opposite a house called Caeser's Corner, named after the builder who extended the cottage, formerly a bakery. The date 1867 is prominently displayed in bottle bottoms on the front of the house.

❻ Turn right, passing Hazelbank Nursery, and then left along Squire's Hill Lane. There are extensive views from here over the wooded countryside. Continue past houses and then dip down past the very pretty Wey Cottage which has a splendid display of delphiniums in the summer. Soon after this turn left down a surfaced footpath. However, it is worth walking on a little to admire the elegant Tilhill House on the right. Return to follow the footpath downhill alongside fields and the river to the post office. Opposite is Bridge Farm, an early 17th-century central smoke bay house; the chimneys were added later. Turn right over the bridge to the Barley Mow and the start of the walk. Don't miss Cobbett's oak at the corner of the green past the pub and near the second river bridge.